SPIRITUAL SINKHOLES

Avoiding the Debilitating Effects of
Compassion Fatigue in Church Leadership.

by

Dr. Jim Caruso

Spiritual Sinkholes:
Avoiding the Debilitating Effects of Compassion Fatigue in Church Leadership.
by Dr. Jim Caruso

Printed in the United States of America

ISBN 9781613798058

Contact the Author at:
jim@jimcarusoconsulting.com
www.jimcarusoconsulting.com

www.xulonpress.com

For my wife Elaine,

my best friend and lifelong learning partner.

ACKNOWLEGEMENTS

An author writes a book in concert with a support team. I acknowledge Janet Anderson who encouraged me to take this to the next level. Other team members include the facilitators and professors at George Fox Evangelical Seminary in Portland, Oregon.

Loren Kerns is a master of encouragement. Shelia Bartlett was the first person I talked with when registering and her friendly encouragement set the stage. Dee Small looked after the administrative components of the program, and I am truly grateful to Dr. Len Sweet for creating a stimulating learning environment. Dr. Chuck Conniry is a great mentor and influenced me from the moment I met him. Dr. Ken Ross has been my advisor from the beginning and has guided me with great expertise and Dr. Larry Day, my expert advisor and immediate friend. Others on the writing team are members of my cohort. You are the best! A finer crew is hard to find. My writing team includes editors Bill Badke, and James and Hannah Dean who repaired, suggested changes, and made the book readable. I am truly grateful to all.

I acknowledge my wife Elaine who is my lifelong learning partner, best friend, best critic, and best encourager. She has enough discipline for both of us and is my best source of encouragement. My daughter Leslie and her husband Jaz Ghag, and my son Dan and his wife Melissa were great support on this journey.

CONTENTS

INTRODUCTION

Houston, we've had a problem.[1]

John Swigert Jr. Apollo 13

Twenty-first century church leadership is bleeding, and clergy in North America are leaving their pulpits at an alarming rate. James Dobson in newsletter April 2009 puts a number on this exodus, "We estimate that approximately 1,500 pastors leave their assignments each month, due to moral failure, spiritual burnout or contention within their local congregations."[2] These statistics cross all denominational lines.

> "Fifteen hundred pastors leave the ministry each month due to moral failure, spiritual burnout or contention in their churches."

Compassion fatigue is a significant contributing factor behind this leadership loss. Pastors, counselors, and other church leaders need to understand its signs and symptoms and avoid personal destruction. Compassion fatigue identifies a serious condition brought on by stress and lack of Sabbath rest. This condition causes many to leave the ministry, and others continue to function but at ineffective levels. These are running on empty. Compassion fatigue affects pastors, their families, and their congregations.

Stress is a natural reaction to any "pleasant or unpleasant [demand] placed upon it."[3] It is not always a negative condition, and we perceive an event based on our attitudes. We experience something as pleasant or positive stress, unpleasant or negative stress, or as neutral stress. Hans Selye describes negative stress as distress, defined as suffering or a state of danger. It is what most people commonly mean when they say someone is stressed. He labeled positive stress as eustress from the Greek prefix for good.[4]

Everyone experiences stress throughout life. Winning the lottery, graduating from school, being chosen for the team or being hired for a coveted position creates eustress. The loss of a loved one, a broken relationship, moving away from friends, downsizing, or losing your career creates distress. Negative stress can affect your body and mind, cause fatigue, impaired judgment, and physical, emotional, and psychological disorders.

Stressors

Negative stress has many sources in caregivers' lives. Burnout is a condition in which the body becomes physically and emotionally exhausted from work conditions and the pressures of serving emotionally needy individuals. Stress can become overwhelming and caregivers shift their focus from the needy to the stress they create. Critical Incident Stress (CIS) is "any incident that we experience which is sudden, unexpected, disturbing and which can

> Compassion fatigue is "the cost of caring for others in emotional pain."

interfere with the ability to function. It is a common reaction, in normal persons, to abnormal situations."[5] This stress can affect caregivers' lives and careers.

Post Traumatic Stress Disorder (PTSD) identifies another type of stress. PTSD is described as "a psychiatric disorder that can occur following the experience or witnessing of life-threatening events such as military combat, natural disasters, terrorist incidents, serious accidents or violent personal assaults like rape."[6] It may occur if individuals do not receive help after a traumatic event. Compassion fatigue develops in response to CIS, PTSD, and many other stressors.

Charles Figley describes compassion fatigue as "the cost of caring for others in emotional pain."[7] In *Compassion Fatigue,* he explains that, "Professionals who listen to clients' stories of fear, pain, and suffering may feel similar fear, pain, and suffering because they care."[8] Later, I will explain compassion fatigue's dynamics and describes its effects on pastors and church leaders.

Life requires balance, and God gave his followers a prescription for avoiding compassion fatigue. His prescription is found in the fourth commandment of the Decalogue; it is observance of the Sabbath. Longevity and peak performance happen when church leaders follow a balanced lifestyle that includes a Sabbath rest. Lack of Sabbath rest is a key component of compassion fatigue among Christian leaders. Ironically, these leaders use the fourth commandment to counsel others, but neglect it in their own lives. I will address the need for Sabbath rest and how to incorporate it into church leaders' lives.

Leadership is crucial. Many seminars and seminary courses emphasize leadership and leadership skills, and strong leadership is essential. The church and the corporate world need Holy Spirit-empowered and directed leaders. Jesus' leadership style differs from many twenty-first century leadership models used in contemporary churches. Sadly, many church models are simply modified corporate hierarchal structures reworked to fit the church. The gospel accounts do not describe Jesus as a New Testament CEO. He was a shepherd-facilitator who equipped his team and acted as a servant leader.

Twenty-first century corporate executives control and direct all organizational functions. However, Jesus is different. He is the *head* of the church, (Eph. 1:22, 1 Cor. 11:3) and the church is Christ's body. Yet Jesus does not lead his team from the highest organizational office. In fact, He leads from the bottom as a servant.

I will describe how the model of hierarchal leadership

> "Why don't we care for ourselves as we care for others?"

structure adds stress and promotes compassion fatigue among church leaders. I believe church leaders are uniquely susceptible to compassion fatigue because they are keen to fulfill "the call to minister." They believe they must give "all they have and all they are" to those they serve, much like martyrs for a cause.

The idea of "being poured out as a drink offering to the Lord" (Phil. 2:17), can be taken improperly by church leaders. Church leaders may neglect self-care and fall into the messiah trap. This may pro- voke addictive behaviors, which

> Compassion fatigue dynamics affect pastors and church leaders.

can result in the church leaders' self-destruction, and can harm their families and those they serve. I have known pas- tors and caregivers who abandoned ministry because they were spent emotionally. Most or all felt guilt and shame because they left their calling and believe they failed God.

I wrote this book for church leaders who may experi- ence compassion fatigue. The threat of compassion fatigue among church leaders is enhanced through exposure to numerous images and stories of trauma, disaster, and death. Compassion fatigue recognition and symptom awareness are crucial for stressed church leaders. Equally important is to know that compassion fatigue is treatable.

I believe leaders must answer a difficult question: "Why don't we care for ourselves as we care for others?" Self- care is essential for church leaders who seek longevity in ministry and healthy personal lives with family and friends. Regular physical exercise is critical to stress management, and the body needs fuel like other machines. Unhealthy food, like poor grades of gasoline or contaminated fuels, interferes with the human machine's performance. The body functions at its best, maintains strength and power, and heals and restores through proper exercise and diet combined with emotional and spiritual balance.

The declaration, "Houston, we have a problem!" resulted from a ruptured oxygen tank while the astronauts orbited the moon. The mission shifted immediately from a moon landing to a repair problem and safe journey home. The ground crew and astronauts shared information and tasks, worked together, and brought the flight crew home safely. Their process serves as an object lesson for church leaders.

I wrote this book to help you flourish in your ministry and prevent the debilitating effects of compassion fatigue. It provides church leaders a "Biblical Preventive Maintenance Plan." It involves sharing information and tasks, working with the Creator, fulfilling your call, and maintaining health and balance.

Shabbat
Relax and Re-Create

You will find opportunities to ponder what you have read at the end of each chapter.

Please stop . . . Shabbat, and take a few minutes.

Relax . . . assume a posture of separation unto God. And re-create . . . meditate on your life and your relationship with God.

CHAPTER ONE

HEADS UP: STRESS COMING IN!

We are inherently not great at taking care of ourselves, —
while we take great pride in our ability to help others.
Jim Lanier[9]

I served in pastoral ministry for twenty-five years and suffered burnout from stressors I did not recognize or understand. As a result I took a two-year hiatus from ministry. Ten years after my burnout experience, I learned that my friend John, from a previous church I pastored, had passed away. Memories of our times together and the difficulties we faced as pastor and friend brought many tears. Deep inside I knew that I could not officiate at his funeral, and I felt an intense reaction at the prospects of offering care to the family at this difficult time.

The next day a second call came; another friend Nathan, from the same congregation, had terminal cancer and would die within a few days. Years ago, I had been Nathan's counselor and he became a follower of Christ. His conversion freed him from a painful, addictive lifestyle, and he became a different person with newfound hope and freedom.

Ironically, I had registered for a seminar held in my friends' community. My first friend's family asked me to officiate at his funeral service. I agreed and thought I would also visit my cancer-stricken friend before he passed away. My wife and I decided we'd leave a couple of days before the seminar. This would give me time to attend the funeral and visit my friend, Nathan, who was under hospice care. I could not sleep the night before we left and awoke feeling weary and empty. I knew I could not officiate or attend the funeral. I lacked the emotional strength to visit my terminally ill friend, and I had nothing left to give. I was spent.

The previous few months took their toll on my emotional reserves. I pastored a growing church that continually presented new demands and problems. I visited three church members with cancer over the past months and officiated at twelve funerals and three weddings. In the same period I counseled many congregants and community members, attended and facilitated three critical incident stress debriefings for local fire and police departments, and shared my son and daughter-in-law's grief over the miscarriage of their second child. In addition I preached every Sunday, and I knew I was about to break.

I called my former church and said I could not attend the funeral, and my wife and I went to a local recreational area to relax and rest as a self-care step. We explored hiking paths, sat on a bench with a calming view of water and mountains, and we talked about our life, ministry, goals, fears, and stress. We laughed, cried, prayed, and asked God tough questions. We had no schedule and seemingly accomplished nothing productive or tangible. On the drive home I felt rested, but guilty because I had a day off.

I attended the seminar without attending the funeral and as well, did not visit my friend with terminal cancer. I didn't even visit my brother who lived in the same community. I felt a new rush of guilt for missing the funeral and not visiting my dying friend or brother. I did not call either of my friends' families after their funerals and guilt affected my personal life and ministry, and I bore a heavy guilt that eventually affected me and my ministry. I knew I needed to care for my congregation… but I was emotionally running on empty. Ultimately, I realized I suffered from compassion fatigue.

This story is my experience as a church leader. The care giving role of pastors often requires them to pour out their compassion for others as they walk intimately with people through crisis and grief. The load of others' pain, fear, and suffering can be more than pastors can bear alone. Some describe this personal depletion of compassion in the care giver's life as secondary traumatic stress disorder, vicarious traumatization, countertransference, secondary traumatic stress, or compassion fatigue. The condition may have a destructive effect on caregivers. Intense, extended caring can deplete or exhaust the caregiver's compassion reserves. Charles Figley describes the progression of this condition:

> Caring people sometimes experience pain as a direct result of their exposure to others' traumatic material. Unintentionally or inadvertently, this secondary exposure to trauma may cause the helpers to inflict additional pain on the originally traumatized. This situation—call it Compassion Fatigue, Compassion Stress, or Secondary Traumatic Stress—is the natural, predictable, treatable and preventable unwanted consequence of working with suffering people.[10]

A large sinkhole appeared recently in a Vancouver, B.C. street. A water main broke, flushed away material under the pavement, and no one saw the danger before the street collapsed. Nothing supported the asphalt's weight, and the surface collapsed into the sinkhole. The sinkhole analogy describes compassion fatigue. Compassion fatigue empties church leaders of compassion, and they may collapse under pressure. In *Ordering Your Private World*, Gordon McDonald writes about the sinkhole syndrome and church leaders, "who work hard, shouldering massive responsibilities at home, at work and at church. *They are good people, but they are very, very tired!* And thus, they too often live on the verge of a sinkhole-like collapse."[11]

Serious Stress in the Shepherd's Life: Sinkholes

Pastoral ministry is about caring. God calls pastors to shepherd others, and he brings them into intimate, caring proximity with people entrusted to their care. On many occasions, God uses church leaders to help others grow and mature in his love. This privileged position comes at a high cost and may empty the shepherd leaders' compassion reserves. Leaders may fail to replenish their compassion reserves through Sabbath times of refreshment and re-creation in the Lord's presence.

The band, Casting Crowns, sings about a church leader's ministry. The song describes two emotionally connected ministry situations and a pastor's compassionate caring and emotional response:

> The love of her life is drifting away.
> They're losing the fight for another day.
> The life that she's known is falling apart.
> A fatherless home, a child's broken heart,
> You're holding her hand, you're straining for words,
> You're trying to make sense of it all.
> She's desperate for hope, darkness clouding her view,
> She's looking to you.
>
> Just love her like Jesus, carry her to him.
> His yoke is easy; his burden is light.
> You don't need the answers to all of life's questions,
> Just know that he loves her and stay by her side.
> Love her like Jesus.
> Love her like Jesus.
>
> The gifts lie in wait, in a room painted blue.
> Little blessings from heaven would be there soon.
> Hope fades in the night, blue skies turn to gray,
> As the little one slips away.
> You're holding her hand, you're straining for words,
> You're trying to make sense of it all.
> They're desperate for hope, darkness clouding
> their view,
> They're looking to you.
>
> Just love her like Jesus, carry her to him.
> His yoke is easy, his burden is light.

You don't need the answers to all of life's questions,
Just know that he loves her and stay by her side[12].

Compassionate church leaders create environments of comfort and support, and they help alleviate others' pain and suffering. God equips spiritual caregivers and calls them to be his love in action. In *Lament for a Son* Nicolas Wolterstoff writes:

> What do you say to someone who is suffering? Some people are gifted with words of wisdom. For such, one is profoundly grateful. There were many such for us. But not all are gifted in that way. Some blurted out strange, inept things. That's OK too. Your words don't have to be wise. The heart that speaks is heard more than the words spoken. And if you can't think of anything at all to say, just say, "I can't think of anything to say. But I want you to know that we are with you in your grief."[13]

The words spoken during difficult times have two layers. One layer is God's love, and the other is pastoral compassion. Church leaders often give of themselves in emotionally charged situations. If they do not constantly refill and refresh themselves, they deplete their compassion reserves and will be ineffective in ministry and their own lives.

In the natural world, erosion creates sinkholes. Erosion can be subtle and unseen until it removes the underlying supports. It undercuts the pavement that carries a vehicle's weight. In a similar a fashion, compassionate serving undercuts church leaders' own personal emotional, physical, and spiritual strength. The collapse is inevitable when erosion accomplishes its work.

I pastored a small church in a rural area, and God told me he didn't need me in that church. I argued with him. After all I was called, the call was confirmed, and I walked in obedience and faith. God told me he could have called anyone to fill that pastoral

> Suffering explodes in life, and pain scatters like shrapnel.

position. "No," he spoke clearly, "I don't need you there."

I was taken aback. I was called to that church. The congregation voted unanimously for me. My church's district office placed me there. I was confused and upset by God's words, but the Lord continued speaking. He said he didn't *need* me there; but he *wanted* me there. He chose me because he wanted me intimately connected with the people to care for their lives. I heard him say, "I will Shepherd the church, and I want you to be the undershepherd." This call was a delicate and vulnerable place for me. In this position, I became enmeshed in people's lives and experienced their emotional stress and challenging journeys. Pastors are called to this privileged position.

In *Five Smooth Stones,* Eugene Peterson discusses suffering and he helped me understand pastors' susceptibility to compassion fatigue. Peterson describes the serious cost of involvement in another's suffering, "When a pastor encounters a person in trouble, the first order of pastoral ministry is to enter into the pain and to share the suffering. . . . Suffering explodes in a life, and pain is scattered like shrapnel."[14] Peterson continues, "It is not the task of the pastor to alleviate suffering, to minimize it, or to mitigate it, but to share it after the example of our Lord Messiah: Surely he hath borne our grief and carried our sorrows."[15]

> Compassion causes us to hurt when others hurt.

Suffering extracts compassion from those created in God's image and sensitive to his Holy Spirit. This is a good and yet troubling reality. It is good because sufferers have compassionate companions on painful journeys. The troubling part is that compassionate companions witness and feels the victims' torments and fears. Peterson writes, "The pastor who substitutes cheery bromides for companionship 'through the valley of deep shadows,' can fairly be

> We sustain life artificially via machines and drugs that were considered science fiction a few years ago.

accused of cowardice. Writing cheerful graffiti on the rocks in the valley of deep shadows is no substitute for companionship with the person who must walk in darkness."[16]

Peterson is correct. Compassionate caregivers often speak positively and hopefully because they are uncomfortable with others' suffering. However, we may obstruct their journey into God's profound presence. Personally, I want to do more than speak positively and hopefully; I want to draw happy faces with florescent paint.

Compassionate people hurt when others hurt, and empathic pastors suffer with those on their journey. The lesson is that God accompanies suffering travelers and does not tire. Pastors, on the other hand, must know when to stop at rest areas. We must take time to re-create ourselves, rest and refresh ourselves in Jesus, and then rejoin those who are suffering. Again, God doesn't *need* us there; he *wants* us there.

What Happened to the Little House on the Prairie Community?

I concluded after twenty-five years of ministry in different sized churches that ministry is more complicated and more stressful than I first thought. Stress invades every area of North American culture including the church. The family is attacked, the biblical view of marriage is challenged, and moralities are shaded in grey. Powerful secular and church leaders fall into immorality, and some leaders lie in their own defense and are found guilty. Many observers question the credibility and integrity of everyone in leadership, Christians and non-Christians alike.

Time and energy saving devices in the twenty-first century have not lessened the effects of stress on our lives. Instead, it seems that progress generates stress. Our society runs at full speed, and many couples work two jobs and place children in daycare. We commute to work. The media and the threat of terrorism intrude constantly. Adult children must help elderly parents make decisions about retirement homes, care homes, and the possibility of three generations living together. These complications produce stress and compassion fatigue.

Emptiness results when compassion and concern drain our emotions, energy, and strength. This creates compassion fatigue. Charles Figley describes this phenomenon as "the cost of caring too much."[17]

Advances in medical care make the contemporary world more complex. Respirators and induced comas have benefits, but there is a downside. Patients' families experience emotional demands and uncertain futures that drain their energy. Medications and bio-replacements extend the life of some body parts, while others deteriorate. The body may be strong, but the mind may deteriorate; the mind may be strong, but the body disabled. Some individuals require constant care that creates stressful emotional demands.

I am not against modern medical discoveries. These breakthroughs extend our loved ones' lives, but the emotional cost can be high.

Living in an iPod World

Technology adds to compassion fatigue. Caregivers' compassion fatigue increases through constant exposure to trauma, disaster, and death. Technical communication advances carry the news up front and center. Our eyes and ears transmit the horror to our brains, and we respond with compassion or desensitization. Memories are triggered and individuals may experience things vicariously. Aphrodite Matsakis writes, "Unlike non-traumatic memories, traumatic memories can bring to the surface not only the images of the event, but the feelings, sounds, smells and bodily states associated with the event."[18]

Germaine Greer expresses her fear about the media in an article about hunger in Africa, "The Four Horsemen[19] are up and away, with the press corps stumbling along behind. . . . At breakfast and at dinner, we can sharpen our own appetites with a plentiful dose of the pornography of war, genocide, destitution and disease."[21] An unnatural amount of global, real-time horror depletes our compassion reserves. This depletion results from cumulative stress whether the events are near or distant. Individuals connected strongly with sufferers are likely candidates for compassion fatigue.

We ate supper and watched Desert Storm unfold in living color. The images were real-time events of full-scale war on the other side of the world. I watched the war from beginning to end, commented on what I saw, and grew tired of the images and horror. This was my first experience of media-related compassion fatigue.

Trauma, war, and human-made and natural disasters fill our history. Why do they seem overwhelming now? The world has become smaller. We live in a global village compared with a vast and expansive older world that took years to circumnavigate. We hear and see events in real time compared with earlier periods when communication was difficult, delayed, or impossible.

We watched the earthquake-spawned tsunami that devastated Thailand, Sri Lanka, and Indonesia. We saw footage of drowning people, anguished survivors, and thousands of corpses in plain view. News reports indicated 250,000 deaths. Compassion fatigue can occur as people around the world watch traumatic events unfold in their living rooms.

People ask, "How do we handle this?" Carol Ostrom writes in *The Seattle Times*:

> Some think this type of terrorism happens only in Ireland, the Middle East, Bosnia, or Sudan.

The images rush into our lives: a terrified Bosnian orphan behind a bullet-riddled bus window; a desperate Somalian mother and her stick-thin staving child. Tragedies everywhere, filling the newspaper pages and television screens. Our hearts and minds struggle like a frantic warzone doctor in a crowded medical tent as the cries for help inundate us. Which hands reaching out for us shall we take, which can we pass by? Should we, who can afford double lattes and extravagant air shows by the Blue Angels, help everyone? Or should we-personally and nationally-perform ethical and psychological triage, deciding which victims of human suffering we will help and which ones we will ignore? Or should we just give in to the impulse to succumb to "compassion fatigue" and pull the all cotton premium goose down covers over our head?[21]

Newsweek had front-page coverage and articles about the 2004 tsunami. One article showed a picture of bodies wrapped and lying on blue tarps and the caption below it said, "Relief workers warn that the death toll from Sunday's disaster could top 50,000."[22] The article included a plethora of traumatic images that the author called "a tragedy in photos."[23]

The number of dead far exceeded the first estimates. The *Newsweek* coverage uses powerful imagery in its introduction, and the article's title declares, "Earthquake's Size, Damage Called Biblical."[24] The picture below the headlines captures the tsunami wave and debris in its destructive wake.

In *Compassion Fatigue: How the Media Sells Disease, Famine, War and Death*, Susan Moeller claims the media creates an avenue for compassion fatigue through instant TV and Internet exposure. We can be overwhelmed by the images, like Daniel Defoe who wrote in 1721, "We had no such thing as printed newspapers in those days to spread rumors and reports of things, and to improve them by the invention of men, as I have lived to see practiced since."[25]

We are bombarded with media coverage of hurricanes in the United States, death and destruction in Iraq and Afghanistan, and misery among hundreds of thousands. The local media adds dinner hour stories about mine disasters and potential "9/11 like" terrorist strikes.

Terror

Osama Bin Laden threatens terror. His threats add stress and fear to a society with memories of 9/11 still on their minds. This new stressor challenges church leaders. Pastors become involved emotionally in people's lives, some of whom may become self-destructive. Compassion fatigue affects emergency caregivers, and others connect with the constant trauma and tragedy in our world. Compassion fatigue increases when reports of terrorist crises appear on our televisions and the Internet.

Oprah Winfrey interviewed a thirty-year-old woman from Rwanda who survived her country's horrific genocide. She watched as killers hacked to death all sixteen of her family members before her eyes. The soldiers who killed her family raped her repeatedly. She escaped death because they wore themselves out. She became pregnant from this rape, kept the baby, and adopted two other children whose parents perished. This story echoes hundreds of other tragic stories from Bosnia, Somalia, Russia, and the United States.

People around the world experience terror while we eat dinner, enjoy freedom, and assure ourselves that we are safe. September 11, 2001, changed our sense of safety. Steven N. Gold and Jan Faust write:

> As many have already noted, the events of September 11th ushered in a new era. The attacks on the Pentagon and the World Trade Center, and the subsequent threat of acts of biological, chemical, and nuclear warfare, immediately and drastically created a shift in perspective among people around the globe. The constantly looming specter of sudden, large-scale terrorist assaults arouses the potential for a type of trauma that is relatively new and about which, therefore, little is known. Traumatologists were just beginning to refine their understanding of how to effectively respond to disasters such as those that occurred at Columbine High School and in Oklahoma City.[26]

People around the world felt 9/11's impact. Gordon Turnbull, a professor of psychology from the United Kingdom responds to Lenore Meldrum's question concerning the impact of 9/11 on people having sought professional help. Turnbull writes:

There is a widely held apprehension in the UK that there will be more terrorist attacks and that some of these will likely be aimed at the UK. Fears that this will be likely to occur have been reinforced by the strong philosophical and practical support that was given to the US in the campaign against the Taliban regime in Afghanistan. There is a strong support for the action in Afghanistan.[27]

Ofra Ayalon is an internationally renowned traumatologist in Kiriat Shmona, Israel. She studies the traumatic effects of terrorism and

> We have become "hyper vigilant" as a global community.

has extensive experience in a nation where terrorism is common. She comments:

It is very well known that the aim of terrorism is not just the numbers of casualties. It is the infliction of fear and unpredictable impending danger. As a matter of fact, terrorism is meant to demoralize the population, although it doesn't always succeed in doing that. The aim of terrorism is to win the psychological war. So, terrorism is like a killing machine in many ways, but its main aims are psychological and political.[28]

Our world will never be the same. The fear of terrorism grows, and the war against this anonymous enemy haunts us. We have become "hyper vigilant" as a global community. We pass through security as we board airplanes, and sky marshals blend in with regular travelers. We know about our vulnerability on trains, subways, at sports events, and in large political gatherings. Life is not the same in the twenty-first century because of terrorism. Life is abnormal, and it may never be normal again. A worldwide vulnerability exists and compassion fatigue results.

Everyday stressors combine with horrific trauma, global terrorism, and more frequent and heinous local crime. Pastors, caregivers, and others experience increased stress. Pastors serve congregational members, conduct weddings and funerals, make hospital visits and court related appearances, counsel victims of childhood sexual abuse, and those who act immorally. How can pastors function under these demands and pressures in their everyday lives? We will look at God's plan for survival in the next chapter.

Shabbat
Relax and Re-Create

Pick up the CD by Casting Crowns or go online and listen to the song: "Love Them Like Jesus." Download or pick up the CD: "Lifesong."

Are you running on empty in your ministry?

Is your life out of control? Talk to someone.

When was the last time you took time off for

yourself?

What fears do you have?

CHAPTER TWO

SINKHOLES

In the feelings of numbing fatigue, a taste of apparent failure, or the bitter experience of disillusionment about goals or purposes, we may have sensed something within us about to give way.[29]
—Gordon MacDonald, *Ordering Your Private World*

Sabbath neglect by pastors and leaders contributes directly to compassion fatigue and related illnesses, and may interfere with a pastor's call from God. The pressures of success, materialism, job security, and time management replace the peace and rest offered in the Lord's presence. Success drives the North American culture and pulls the church into its web.

Pastors and leaders are driven to prove their religious success through church growth, building programs, and increased budgets. Many never achieve these goals because they exhaust their resources and do not take Sabbath rest in the Lord's presence. Others fall into tragic sinkholes. Church leaders deplete their emotional reserves and experience compassion fatigue.

Lack of Sabbath rest erodes church leaders' emotional reserves and forms sinkholes, but pastors can follow biblical directives and avoid sinkholes and the debilitating effects of compassion fatigue. If church leaders live unhealthy lifestyles they may be drawn toward damaging attractions that affect their lives and leadership negatively.

Medical/Psychological Intervention

Compassion fatigue depletes the caregiver of empathy and compassion, and this may lead to depression that requires psychotherapy and medications. Archibald Hart explains how the process works in depressed persons, "The (antidepressant) medication helps to deal with the acute symptoms and the counseling (or psychotherapy) re-orders the longstanding characterological or behavioral problems that either precipitate or aggravate the depression."[30]

When the brain is depleted of certain neural transmitters, it has difficulty repairing itself. The medications increase neural transmitters levels and restore brain function. Once the chemical balance is restored, counseling helps identify the root causes of the psychological damage. Medications and counseling help restore depressed persons' health.

Self-Medication

Anti-depressant medication is non-addictive, but other medications are addictive including sleeping pills, tranquilizers, and narcotics. According to the University of Alberta's website, "It is estimated that more than one million Canadians are addicted to the prescription medications that were meant to heal them. The problem is widespread; some addiction specialists say five times as many Canadians are addicted to medications than are hooked on heroin or cocaine."[31] These statistics show the serious risks of handling personal problems with unsupervised pharmaceuticals and the difficulty of breaking dependence.

Pain tells us something is seriously wrong. As such, pain can be a good thing because it alerts us of the need for evaluation and resolution. Many church leaders are motivated by compassion, and they may suffer others' pain vicariously. Webster defines compassion as "a feeling of deep sympathy and sorrow for another who is stricken by suffering or misfortune, accompanied by a strong desire to alleviate the pain or remove its cause." [32] Compassion requires empathy. Caregivers who empathize with traumatized persons understand the person's experience of trauma, but the caregivers may become traumatized. Carl Rogers defined empathy:

> [Empathy is] entering the private perceptual world of the other and becoming thoroughly at home in it. It involves being sensitive, moment to moment, to the changing felt meanings which flow in this other person, to the fear or rage or tenderness or confusion or whatever, that he/she is experiencing. It means temporarily living in his/her life, moving about in it delicately without making judgments, sensing meanings of which he/she is scarcely aware, but not trying to uncover feelings of which the person is totally unaware, since this would be too threatening. It includes communicating your sensing of his/her world as you look with fresh and unfrightened eyes at elements of which the individual is fearful. [33]

When church leaders move beyond empathy into unhealthy identification with sufferers, they may be injured and experience compassion fatigue.

Feelings of emptiness, helplessness, guilt, and extreme exhaustion may push church leaders toward unhealthy, pain numbing solutions. They may seek relief through self-medication with alcohol, prescription drugs, or even illegal drugs. As stress increases church leaders may become addicted to these numbing agents. Repetition leads to dependence and dependence to addiction. In *Spirituality and Leadership,* Alan Nelson summarizes this destructive path:

> When negative stress continues for a period of time, leaders can begin to cave in from the pressure. Those who haven't learned to resort to spiritual means and faith in God often pursue unhealthy stress reduction; this can be through materialism, an obsession with a hobby, extreme sports, sexual affairs or substance abuse.[34]

When the "cave-in" happens to church leaders, numbing the pain or acquiring external strength may become central for survival, and addiction may follow. Pastors may handle their ministry duties effectively for a while, but they may become prisoners to compulsive needs. The slide into addiction is subtle, and Stephen Arterburn and Jack Felton describe it:

> Addictions develop when people seek relief from pain, a quick fix, or an immediate altered mood. When a person develops a pathological relationship to this

mood-altering experience or substance that has life-damaging consequences, addiction exists. The addict becomes addicted to the source of mood alteration and, by giving up everything for that change in feelings, comes to worship the addictive act with mind body and spirit.[35]

Addicted church leaders cannot fulfill their idealistic ministry dreams, and they become trapped in a vortex of dependence, which is the antipathy of God's peace and stability. This cyclic pattern increases dependence on the addictive behavior and leads to increased feelings of guilt, shame, and failure that perpetuate the unhealthy behavior. The addiction becomes the victims' object of worship, and victims become servants to their addictions. John O'Neill describes addicted persons as follows:

> The professional who on a daily basis may handle multiple critical problems simply may believe he can figure out a way to handle his own problems. When someone is depressed or anxious, he usually looks for a way to feel better, often by self-medicating with alcohol or other addictive behavior. Conversely, after using the person is apt to feel more depressed or anxious, leading to a dangerous cycle in which he feels stuck.[36]

Self-medication can provide short periods of relief for the one involved, but it does not resolve compassion fatigue because it is not God's rest and restoration. The guilt and shame attached to the cyclic action of self-medication adds to stress in church leaders' lives and may cause a return to addictive behavior. Peace and rest remain elusive.

Sexual Sin and Sexual Addiction

Sexual addiction is another way to deal with pain and discouragement in ministry, and some church leaders have fallen into this sinkhole. Recently, the world became aware of Ted Haggard's sexual involvement with another man. The man sold Haggard methamphetamines, which Haggard claims he threw away. Haggard confessed in a letter to his church and the National Association of Evangelicals, of which he was president, "There is part of my life that is so repulsive and dark that I've been warring against it all of my adult life."[37]

Haggard's story is not new. In the early 1980s, Jimmy Swaggart and Jim Bakker succumbed to sexual sin and left their ministries in disgrace. Amie Semple McPherson left her ministry under a cloud of suspicion of sexual immorality, and Catherine Kuhlman was involved in an adulterous affair while in ministry. Protestant and Catholic church leaders commit sexual sins, and the size of the church is not a contributing factor. I dealt with staff members' moral failures in a small church. I'm personally aware of eight moral failures of leaders of different sized churches within one denomination during a period of fewer than eight months.

Why is sexual sin a failure among church leaders? All leaders have charisma and attract those who seek someone to follow. Leaders personify confidence, take risks, accomplish things, and confront conflict. Church leaders may also love others unconditionally, demonstrate spiritual prowess, and listen well with sympathy, empathy, and grace. If God has gifted the church leader with a striking physical appearance, this can become a lethal recipe for moral failure.

Gordon MacDonald is a fallen pastor and one time president of InterVarsity Christian Fellowship. His story illustrates the vulnerability O'Neill describes. Before MacDonald committed adultery, he was asked, "If Satan were to destroy you, how would he accomplish such a feat?" MacDonald answered, "All sorts of ways, I suppose; but I know there's one way he wouldn't get me. . . . He'd never get me in the area of my personal relationships. That's one place where I have no doubt that I'm as strong as you can get."[38] A few years later his world fell apart. MacDonald cautions leaders,

"An unguarded strength and an unprepared heart are double weakness."[39]

In extreme situations, church leaders who overwork and experience emotional erosion may seek unhealthy ways to reduce stress. This may lead them into hedonistic pursuits or into addictive behaviors that provide a sense of peace and freedom from pain. *This may involve addictive sexuality.*

Thaddeus Birchard describes the isolating effect of sexual addiction on individuals in "The Snake and the Seraph — Sexual Addiction and Religious Behaviour":

> Sexual behaviors are used addictively to control painful affect, to avoid feelings of loneliness, and to ward off the dread of non-being. Once the behaviour begins, he/she is out of pain and out of reality for the duration of the episode. A tunnel closes around the addict and nothing exists and nothing much matters but the pursuit of the behaviour. However bad life seems after the behaviour — loneliness, anxiety and shame are banished for the duration.[40]

Sexual addiction can be used to deal with the pain and discouragement of ministry. Birchard explains a possible connection between sexual addiction and its propensity in highly stressed church leaders:

> Religious behaviour and sexual behaviour can come from the same place. They can both be responses to narcissistic damage. This is, I believe, the key to

understanding much of the professional misconduct and the combined appearance in clients of religious and sexual behaviors that alternate, or are perceived to be in conflict, but are held at the same time. The co-existence of these two patterns, explain splitting, create high levels of shame and requirements for secrecy, all of which fuel the processes of painful affect, low self-esteem and self-contempt.[41]

Sally Morgenthaler concludes in her article, "Does Ministry Fuel Addictive Behavior?" "Image-driven pastors learn how to edit their real lives for public consumption. In the heat of stress or in the wear and tear of the mundane, the veneer will wear through to what is really there."[42] The veneer, when removed, reveals an emotional sinkhole caused by ministry stress, and compassion fatigue results.

Hedonism

Culture in North America changed drastically after the Second World War. This created "must have" and "constantly busy" self-gratification seekers with insatiable appetites for new technological products. Lyle Schaller identifies the impact societal changes had on culture during the mid twentieth century:

The generations born before 1935 grew up in a world that placed a premium on the sense of community. . . . The generations born after 1955 have grown up in a culture that is organized around choices, competition, quality, large scale institutions, rapid change, innovations, convenient parking, surprises, a non-geographical basis for creating social networks, anonymity, complexity, discontinuity with the past and the drive of the new consumerism.[43]

Materialism became an object of worship.

Both church and secular leaders face the debilitating effects of compassion fatigue, and they pursue "something" to fill the void caused by compassion fatigue. This "something" can lead to hedonism defined as "buying pleasurable experiences and collectables, and/or encountering a false psycho-spirituality such as meditation, visualization or positive confession ."[44]

Hunger for pleasure as an anesthetic permeates our sacred and secular societies because sacred and secular societies seek relief. Many times the lines of demarcation are blurred and both groups find themselves using spirituality and hedonism to fill the void. Type "hedonism" into the Google search engine on the Internet and the results include ads for hedonistic resorts and super clubs designed for adults and their pleasure satisfaction.

Church leaders are susceptible to this self-gratifying desire for pleasure. Jim Bakker created Heritage USA in the early 1980s as a theme park for Christians. He advertised it as a place where Christian families could go on holiday free from tobacco and obscene language as they ate meals and relaxed by the pool in the gated community. The concept was to create a Christian theme park that would rival existing theme parks created for pleasure and relaxation. The park was hedonism in the name of Christianity:

> [T]he Fort Mill site was over 2000 acres. To give you an idea of the size, you could fit the original Disneyland, UK's Blackpoll Pleasure Beach, Six Flags Great America, and Universal Studio's Florida all inside the grounds together, and still have enough room left over to add Cedar Point, Knott's Berry Farm, and little old Geauga Lake, Ohio. . . . In other words, it's big. At one point during the "life" of Heritage, over 6 million people were visiting the park during the year. If I'm not mistaken, (the writer's comment), a well-known park like Cedar Point here in Ohio gets around 3 million. I think Disney gets more like 12 or 15 million, but obviously 6 million is a huge number for an upstart like Heritage. [45]

Hedonism became a source of healing after the attack on the World Trade Center in 2001, and the President of the United States of America preached hedonism's message.

Benjamin Barber writes, "President Bush squandered a great opportunity when the nation cried out for engagement [after 9/11] and the president . . . urged them to go shopping. . . . To relinquish fear people must step out of paralysis. The president suggested they step into the mall."[46] In our culture, we look to materialism for status, happiness, comfort, renewed self-esteem, and relief from depression, grief, and loss.

The opposite is true. No amount of material gain or hedonistic pleasure could reestablish security or confidence after the 9/11 terrorist attack. Materialism numbs pain and brings instant gratification, as do drugs addicts use for pain relief or instant euphoria. Temporary fixes, however, do nothing to fix the fundamental problem. It only pushes it back until the drug wears off. The problem reappears, combined with a new set of problems related to use of the drug. A cycle of addiction ensues and the real issue remains. The rich young man possessed an abundance of material wealth, but he was incomplete. Jesus told him to stop indulging in materialism, sell his possessions, give to the poor, and follow him (Matt. 19:16-26).

At the time I write this, the world is experiencing a global economic meltdown. Nations are dealing with recession, job cuts, and bank and investment firm failures. Longstanding multi-billion dollar corporations seek bankruptcy, and unemployment grows by the tens of thousands. The foreclosure rate is overwhelming and many people lose the material gains they accumulated during the bull market. Our solution is to give trillions of dollars in loans and grants to the business and investment sectors and encourage people to spend more. Pleasure still reigns as a god.

Spiritual Alternatives

Many people express interest in alternative religions that offer meditative courses on how to slow down, rest, and connect peacefully with body, soul, and spirit. Meditation and visualization for inner peace and rest are a spiritual repackaging of Eastern religion, and hundreds of thousands of North American people participate in them. The spiritual emphasis includes many different gods, and Jesus is accepted as one of the idolatrous conglomeration, but not the only God.

For example, I attended a secular seminar on compassion fatigue. Part way through the facilitator asked participants to engage in a relaxation exercise. The words were calming and his voice soothing. He asked participants to meditate and visualize a happy thought or a safe and happy place. Next, he asked us to relax. He suggested we invite all our body parts to cease tension and begin rest, starting with the head and neck and naming each part of our bodies successively. As the relaxation progressed, the facilitator instructed partici-pants to talk with their inner guides, gently reminding them-selves they were their own healers and sources of power and life. Individuals in high stress occupations, including emer-gency personnel, police, physicians, CEOs and all levels of management and sales personnel attend these self-centered seminars.[47]

In the past, the church was the authority on social and spiritual knowledge sought by the majority of people in North America. The church steeple stood higher than any other structure in the community. This changed when other spiritual groups offered access to peace and rest for restless people engaged in North America's constantly changing cul-ture. For example, Annie Besant aspires to eradicate worry through thought power, "Let, then, a person, who is suf-fering from worry, give three or four minutes in the morning, on first rising, to some noble and encouraging thought, 'The Self is Peace; that Self is Strength; that Self am I.'"[48] Schmidt writes, "[A]cross the board, meditation was her-alded as a salve for anxiety and as an unrivaled source of serenity."[49] Use of meditation and alternative spiritual exercises increased exponentially as the demands of modern day stress and busyness spin out of control. Anxiety and a lack of peace combine with a shortage of time and draw many into non-biblical healing for their out-of-control lives. These solutions are not Christ centered, but it appeals to many tired people caught in stress, anxiety, and depression. These solutions are counterfeit to the real peace and rest found in Christ. Meditating on other gods, whatever their origin, is a violation of the first commandment.

The North American culture is spinning out of control through busyness and stress. Our society no longer values the church's influence in everyday life. The church also has changed, and church leaders send confusing messages to persons seeking spiritual answers to everyday life questions. Church leaders tire, some leave the church, and others become addicted to drugs, sex, or a variety of other destructive practices. Others become materialistic or embrace non-biblical religious practices. As a result their lives lack spiritual strength and adequate resources and they experience compassion fatigue. The following chapter offers God's plan for compassion fatigue.

Shabbat
Relax and Re-Create

When was the last time you had a complete physical exam? Is there something that is bothering you (fear, pain, depression) that you have not discussed with anyone?

Who is your sounding board? Who do you talk with for self-care? Do you need to talk with them now?

Go to the end of the book and look at the Appendix. Take the ProQOL R-V 5 (Professional Quality of Life: Compassion Satisfaction and Fatigue Subscales.) Read the scoring instructions carefully. How did you do? Are you in need of a rest? Are you satisfied with your work? Do you need a lifestyle change? Are you in Burnout?

Read: Carmen Rene Berry, When Helping You is Hurting Me: Escaping the Messiah Trap (New York: The Crossroad, 2003).

What safeguards have you implemented in your ministry when ministering to or counseling with the opposite sex?

Are you investing in your marriage relationship regularly? When was the last time you dated your spouse? Marriage conferences are a great investment in your relationship; make plans to attend one within the next few months.

How large an influence is materialism in your life? Do you over spend when you are emotionally depleted?

How much time do you spend in personal devotions? Is Christ the center of your life? Your marriage? Your family? Your ministry?

CHAPTER THREE

REST AREA AHEAD

There is a day
When the road neither
Comes nor goes, and the way
Is not a way, but á place.[50]
Wendell Berry

It was a few days before Christmas. Usually my wife and I invite widows and other lonely people to our home Christmas day for presents, games, fellowship, and a wonderful turkey and ham dinner. The house fills up. Many times the number of guests does not allow for a meal at the table, so the visitors balance their full plates on their knees and sit throughout our home.

This year was different. We didn't invite anyone, and we didn't accept any Christmas day invitations. We decided to be alone on Christmas day. Our children and grandkids would arrive on Boxing Day, and we postponed Christmas dinner until then. We headed home from the church after the candlelight service on Christmas Eve, exchanged a few gifts, and went to sleep. Christmas day arrived as usual, but the day unfolded very differently from other Christmas days. My wife enjoys sleeping in, so I rose at about seven o'clock, put on the coffee, and picked up the Christmas gift she gave me the night before, a book written by John Grisham.

I read, ate breakfast, read some more, fell asleep, and the cycle continued until eleven o'clock that evening. Throughout the day my wife did what she wanted. We chatted and napped and ate non-Christmas day meals like peanut butter sandwiches, cereal, and eggs at all times of the day and

> It was Christmas day. I am a pastor, and lonely people need a good meal and companionship.

evening. I finished my book and was rested at the end of the day. I had taken a very short sabbatical.

I felt guilty. It *was* Christmas day. I *am* a pastor, and lonely people need a good meal and companionship, but I knew that I needed a rest. What eased my conscience was that John Grisham is a Christian. I had read a book by a Christian author on one of the most celebrated Christian days.

Sabbath Theology

What is theology and how does it affect us? Ken Radant defines theology, "The Church's attempt to give a coherent explanation of the nature of God and His relationship to the world."[51] Radant's thoughts about theology suggest that as we study about God, he begins to reveal his plan and purpose for us. Acquiring this knowledge through prayer and study of his word teaches us how we please him through a relationship that develops and reveals his truth and direction for his followers personally and corporately. In *Christian Theology,* Millard Erickson suggests that Christians mature in relationship with God when they embrace theology, "Thus theology will also seek to understand God's creation, particularly man and his condition, and God's redemptive working in relation to mankind."[52] Sabbath theology describes God's words about Sabbath and what God requires for observance during Sabbath rest. It considers how the Old and New Testament writers describe the importance of obedience and Sabbath observance. Understanding and applying this theology to one's life in ministry helps avoid the debilitating effects of CF.

My one day off to feel rested was an anomaly for me, but God's Sabbath day's rest is a healthy idea. In 2008, Christine Sine spoke at a workshop about how God's rhythms provide stability and flexibility. She said, "Life is essentially God's combination of rhythms that regulate our bodies, souls, and spirits."[54] These rhythms do not add stress; instead, they relieve our stress and provide a healthy framework. Problems arise when our rhythms and routines conflict with God's rhythms and routines. The creation writer says that God finished his creation and declared his work complete, "Thus the heavens and the earth were completed, and all their hosts. By the seventh day God completed his work, which he had done, and he rested on the seventh day from all his work, which he had done. Then God blessed the seventh day and sanctified it, because in it he rested from all his work which God had created and made" (Gen. 2:1 3). God walked in Eden with his human creation and provided a Sabbath environment for creature and Creator. After the fall, God drove Adam and Eve out of the garden, and humans have tried ever since to rediscover the garden's Sabbath environment.

The Old Testament writers describe how God desired to reestablish his presence and fellowship of presence with his creation as he had in Eden. He set forth the law in the

Decalogue and directed how humans could enter into a relationship with him and his creation. His law included a directive for Sabbath rest, but Humans created Sabbath legalism in response.

The Decalogue provides an important strategy for managing God's call to leadership. God instructs his people how to live in accordance with his plan and their relationships with God and one another. The first four commandments focus on humanity's relationship with God and the following six commandments deal with human relationships. The key for Moses as a leader was the fourth commandment:

> Remember the Sabbath day, to keep it holy. Six days you shall labor and do all your work, but the seventh day is a Sabbath of the LORD your God; in it you shall not do any work, you or your son or your daughter, your male or your female servant or your cattle or your sojourner who stays with you. For in six days the LORD made the heavens and the earth, the sea and all that is in them, and rested on the seventh day; therefore the LORD blessed the Sabbath day and made it holy. (Exod. 20:8-11)

God's ten words were not called commandments in the original text. Dan Block writes, "Contrary to modern practice, the Scriptures never refer to the Decalogue as the 'Ten Commandments.'"[54] The document in both contexts reads, "all these words" (Exod. 20:1, Deut. 5:22) that Yahweh "spoke," rather than "these commandments" that Yahweh "commanded." This document is identified as "the Ten Words" (Exod. 34:28, Deut. 4:13; 10:4) in the Bible, not as "the Ten Commandments."

Moses and the Israelites would live long and productive lives that pleased God and others when they obeyed these words. The idea that these words were given to the Israelites as a guide for life suggests that each "word" has equal value for the hearer.

> The idea that these words were given to the Israelites as a guide for life suggests that each "word" has equal value for the hearer.

Things have not changed for God's people because the Decalogue remains required conduct for those who follow the Lord. Jesus confirmed this when a lawyer asked about the greatest commandment, "You shall love the Lord your God with all your heart, and with all your soul, and with all your mind. This is the great and foremost commandment. The second is like it; you shall love your neighbor as yourself. On these two commandments depend the whole Law and the Prophets" (Matt. 22:37-40).

Jesus' words describe the willingness of the lover to submit completely to the love object. In his first commandment, Jesus' first four words reprise the Decalogue and refer to our vertical relationship with God (Exod. 20:2-11). In his second commandment, Jesus focuses on love for neighbor and refers to the horizontal relationship we have with one another (Exod. 20:12-17). This is a divine directive for self-care because we must have a healthy love and respect for ourselves before we can properly love others. These two commandments do not replace God's commanding words; instead, upon Christ's words hang the whole law and the prophets. Jesus gives his followers insight into the significance of observing the Decalogue's words.

The Old Testament reports two accounts of the Decalogue recorded in Exodus 20 and Deuteronomy 5. In Exodus 20, God reminds the Israelites that God rested following six days of creation work; in Deuteronomy 5, God reminds the Israelites about their deliverance from Egyptian bondage. The words are an invitation to rest:

> Observe the Sabbath day by keeping it holy, as the LORD your God has commanded you. Six days you shall labor and do all your work, but the seventh day is a Sabbath to the LORD your God. On it you shall not do any work, neither you, nor your son or daughter, nor your manservant or maidservant, nor your ox, your donkey or any of your animals, nor the alien within your gates, so that your manservant and maidservant may rest, as you do. Remember that

you were slaves in Egypt and that the LORD your
God brought you out of there with a mighty hand and
an outstretched arm. Therefore, the LORD your God
has commanded you to observe the Sabbath day.
(Deut. 5:12-15)

The Deuteronomy Decalogue recalls the deliverance
of Israel from Egyptian bondage. Buchanan suggests this
reminds us to celebrate freedom from slavery, but not by
working or doing something we believe important. Instead,
God want us to celebrate as God's children freed to rest and
enjoy life:

> You once were slaves. There was once a day you were
> denied any choice in the matter. Rest? Work? There
> was no option. The choice was made for you, day in,
> day out. The point was reinforced by bullwhips, in
> case you missed it or were the least inclined to ignore
> it. The point was, you worked. Period. Rest was for
> other people. Rest was for Pharaoh. But Pharaoh
> couldn't rest if you didn't work—he had ambitions,
> so many things he wanted to accomplish, so many
> tall, pointy monuments he wanted to be remem-
> bered by-someone had to do it. That somebody, that
> nobody was you.[55]

Celebrating freedom from bondage and slavery is rest.
Moses says that God's followers are not slaves driven by the
whip to the point of exhaustion. Instead of the brutal work
that consumes every moment of their lives, they can rest

and enjoy God's creation. God allows us one day a week to accomplish nothing, guilt free, knowing in silence that God's Spirit infuses life into our souls, bodies, and spirits.

Sabbath Observance According to the
Old and New Testaments

What does God expect in our Sabbath observation? The Hebrew word "rested" in Genesis 2:2 is *shabbat*, which means to "cease from," or to "stop." Stopping busyness results in rest and re-creation. Logan lists thirty-nine prohibited works compiled by the rabbis' exegesis of Exodus 35 and Exodus 25:3:

> The main classes of work are forty save one: sowing, plowing, reaping, binding, sheaves, threshing, winnowing, cleansing crops, grinding, sifting, kneading, baking, shearing wool, washing or beating or dyeing it, spinning, weaving, making two loops, weaving two threads, separating two threads, tying, loosening, sewing two stitches, tearing in order to sew two stitches, hunting a gazelle, slaughtering or flaying or salting or curing its skin, scraping it or cutting it up, writing two letters, erasing in order to write two letters, building, pulling down, putting out a fire, lighting a fire, striking with a hammer and taking anything from one domain to another.[56]

The rabbis promoted other Sabbath regulations. For instance, Hebrews could not journey more than 3,000 feet on the Sabbath, and persons caught doing menial tasks such as gathering wood could be stoned (Num. 15:32-36). Rabbis policed the strict Sabbath observance and the penalties for disobedience were severe. Logan writes:

> Sabbath profanation is listed among the offenses punishable by stoning, which was the second-gravest form of capital punishment, after burning, and followed by beheading and strangling—all penalties that the Sanhedrin had power to inflict. Stoning was inflicted only for cardinal offenses against the Sabbath, such as kindling a fire, prescribed in Scripture (Exodus 35:3). But such a penalty was indicated only if there were two or more witnesses to the act, and if the offender were warned. In other words, there had to be deliberate and stubborn intent.[57]

Sabbath observance was a life or death situation. Rabbis added to God's laws and soon it was impossible to do anything on Sabbath without fear of punishment.

What a Difference a Day Makes

My study about Sabbath observance included arguments over the proper Sabbath day. In *Sabbath Theology*, Maurice

Logan discussed whether the Sabbath observance should be on Sunday or Saturday:

> Notice particularly that the Sabbath law does not specify what day of the week is the Sabbath, for any day of the week is the seventh after the six preceding days. Neither does the Creation reason given, when interpreted literally, specifies what day of the week is the Sabbath; for any one day of rest after the six days of work is in accordance with the Creation model given as the reason for blessing the Sabbath.[58]

This issue is the subject of many books and seminars. Perhaps North American Christians spend more time debating the day to observe than they do its proper observance. Logan helps us set a day aside and observe the blessing of Sabbath regardless of the day of week.

Sabbath Is Essential to Life

The Old Testament law directed humans to Sabbath rest that could be experienced by adherence to the law. Jesus does not require his followers to do certain things to qualify for God's rest, but instead Christians can faithfully respond to his invitation, "Come to me . . . and I will give you rest" (Matt. 11:28).

Jesus removed the legal bondage of the Sabbath when he declared to the Pharisees, "The Sabbath was made for man and not man for the Sabbath" (Mark 2:27), and he declared he was the Lord of the Sabbath (Mark 2:28). The idea that Jesus declared this position reminds his followers that he was fully God. Jesus did not declare that he is a master who serves God's the law; instead, he declared that he is God. He leads his followers from a legalistic adherence toward a proper protocol for life following God, the giver of life.

Jesus declares he came to fulfill the law (Matt. 5:16-18), and he is Sabbath rest (Matt. 11:27-29). Sabbath observance changed from obedience for righteousness to a relational invitation where the person of Jesus Christ is rest. In his Lordship of the Sabbath declaration, Jesus broke many sacred Sabbath rules in full-view of the Sabbath-enforcing Sanhedrin and legalistic Pharisees.

Jesus lived out his Sabbath lordship in everyday life. He picked grain and ate it on Sabbath

> "The Sabbath was made for man and not man for the Sabbath."

(Matt. 12:1), healed a man with a withered hand (Matt. 12:10), healed a woman sick for eighteen years (Luke 13:13), healed a man suffering from dropsy (Luke 14), and mixed clay and healed a blind man (John 9:14). Despite all the good

Jesus did on Sabbath his enemies wanted to kill him, "For this reason therefore the Jews were seeking all the more to kill him, because he not only was breaking Sabbath, but also was calling God his own Father, making himself equal with God" (John 5:18). Jesus did not cause conflict intentionally; instead, his actions declared that he was God.

Those opposed to his ministry and his declaration of deity were familiar with the concept of physical needs being met through Sabbath rest. The Pentateuch writers told the story of God who supplied the Israelites manna during their forty-year wilderness journey (Exod. 16). God provided enough manna for six days, and on the sixth day he increased the amount to accommodate the needs of the Sabbath day. Those who collected more than their share during the six days preceding the Sabbath had no excess and those who collected less had no lack (Exod. 16:18). This experience strengthened their faith in the Lord's provision because the extra manna assured them that God would provide. It reinforced the concept that the six days were a time for gathering, and the Sabbath was a time to rest and enjoy what they gathered, without work. The metaphor is a beautiful picture of the Christ.

Jesus declared his Sabbath lordship. He reinforced this declaration when he announced he was the bread of life coming down from heaven (John 6:33-51). The correlation between the manna in the wilderness and Jesus' declaration to his followers and detractors identifies him as the fulfillment of God's provision. Jesus is the Lord of the Sabbath who invites us to enter his rest.

Jesus taught his followers that Sabbath legalism brought bondage and death. Jesus modeled correct Sabbath observance when he separated from the crowds' demands and worldly busyness and spent time in his Father's presence. The Mount of Transfiguration account (Matt. 17:1-8, Luke 9:27-36) provides a glimpse into the rest Jesus experienced in the presence of God. His entrance into God's presence followed an intense ministry of healing, deliverance, and miracles, and this is the first account of what Jesus experienced when he spent time with his Father. Perhaps this occurred each time Jesus withdrew for rest and re-creation, and he may have included the disciples' inner circle so they could experience a refreshing, restful, re-creational, and spiritual Sabbath. He taught his followers to enter God's presence.

Hebrews 4 reminds Christ's followers that they can experience Sabbath rest. In *The Sabbath in the New Testament: Answers to Questions*, Samuele Bacchiocchi writes:

> In the light of the Cross "the Sabbath rest that remains for the people of God" (Heb. 4:9) is not only a physical cessation from work to commemorate God's perfect creation but also a spiritual entering into God's rest (Heb. 4:10) made possible through Christ's complete redemption. The physical act of resting becomes a vehicle through which one experiences the spiritual rest. We cease from our daily work to allow God to work in us more freely and fully.[59]

The writer to the Hebrews reminds believers about Sabbath rest. They must observe Sabbath, and he warns them that failure to do so is disobedience to God and expresses a lack of faith. It is right for Postmodern church members to observe Sabbath. What does a lack of Sabbath observance suggest about the faith of twenty-first century Christians?

> What does a lack of Sabbath observance suggest about the faith of twenty-first century Christians?

Any desire to live our lives or fulfill our call without observing Sabbath rest indicates a lack of trust in God. Those with faith believe God can accomplish all he wishes in pastors' lives while still giving us Sabbath rest.

The Post Modern Church and Sabbath

The Sabbath is a controversial subject. I studied books written as early as 1835 and up to the present day, and their main focus is on the proper day for Sabbath observance. Much less is written about how to observe Sabbath. I see no need to answer the question: "Which day is Sabbath?" Instead we need an answer to the question: "What do we do to observe Sabbath?" In *Celebrating the Sabbath: Finding Rest in a Restless World,* Bruce Ray discusses the church and Sabbath observance. He writes about our busyness and addiction to sports, shopping, traveling, hiking, and even yard work that have priority over a day of re-creation in the Creator's presence.

Believers seek ways to observe Sabbath, but they may legislate Sabbath to prevent anything that might be considered work. As I mentioned earlier, Jewish Sabbath observance

> Pastors and leaders are usually exhausted when worshippers leave and the church is locked up for another Sunday.

became a multitude of rules requiring obedience upon penalty of death. In the Middle Ages, some people believed separation from the world in a cloistered environment was

Sabbath observance. Raymond Blakeny translated Meister Eckhart's writings and wrote about the mystic's views of separation from the world: Meister Eckhart wrote about the benefits of this separation:

> Once in the cloister I said: The true archetype of the soul is revealed when God alone and nothing else can be described or imagined. The soul has two eyes— one looking inwards and the other looking outwards. It is the inner eye of the soul that looks into the essence and takes being directly from God. That is its true function. The soul's outward eye is directed toward creatures and perceives their external forms but when a person turns inwards and knows God in terms of his own awareness of him, in the roots of his being, he is then freed from all creation and is secure in the castle of truth.[60]

Theresa of Avila, Thomas Aquinas, and St. John of the Cross sought this separation from the world. A monastic life-style might seem extreme in our church culture because we interact busily with non-Christians, counsel, visit the sick and lonely, and teach leadership, missions, evangelism, and biblical doctrine. Separation from the world, however, does not solve compassion fatigue.

Pastors or church leaders may not emphasize Sabbath rest because their Sundays are days of preparation, sermon delivery, ministry, counseling, and care for the flock. Pastors and leaders are usually exhausted when worshippers leave and the church is locked up for another Sunday. Ray writes:

> McSabbath is here—worship services that are quick, easy, convenient and user-friendly. No muss, no fuss. Little or no sacrifice required. Consumers can be in and out in under an hour. McSermons may not be as nutritional as the real thing, but, like Big Macs, they have a predictable quality that fills a void at least for awhile. The question is, however, do they fill the purpose of worship, which is to please God?[61]

What happens to the church when we neglect the commandment found in the Old (Exod. 20, Deut. 5) and the New Testaments (Heb. 4)? In *Sabbath Sense: A Spiritual Antidote for the Overworked,* Donna Schaper sounds an alarm, "When we lost the Sabbath, we lost the sacredness of time."[62] Schaper continues:

> Since Sabbath is no longer clearly defined by society's or religion's rules, Sabbath is a discipline we have to make and do ourselves. We have to choose participation—either in formal, structured religious institutions, or in personal or communal spiritual practices of our own. And we have to surmount obstacles that block our regular participation—whether economic or familial. The obstacles also include our own fatigue as we live too many working lives in too short a week. If we do not separate our time, no one will do it for us.[63]

In *Leaving Church,* Barbara Brown Taylor describes this from a clergyperson's perspective:

> Like every other clergyperson I knew, I believed I had no alternative. Taking a full day off was so inconceivable that I made up reasons why it was not possible. If I stopped for a whole day, there would be no weekend weddings at Grace-Calvary, or someone else would have to do them. Sick people would languish in the hospital and begin to question their faith. Parishioners would start a rumor that I was not a real shepherd, but only a hired hand. If I stopped for a whole day, my animals would starve, my house would grow mold, weeds would take over my garden, and my credit rating would collapse.[64]

Church leaders are challenged to jump off the busyness treadmill and become Sabbath observers who are rested and re-created in Christ and examples to their flocks. The writer of Hebrews states, "Let us, therefore, be diligent to enter that same rest, lest anyone fall through following the same example of disobedience?" (Heb. 4:11) If we are too busy doing God's work to enter into his presence, we neglect his invitation and command. The avoidance of Sabbath observance has far reaching physical, spiritual, and emotional consequences for church leaders. Scripture encourages leaders to observe the Sabbath rest and receive benefits, rejuvenation, and re-creation.

Church leaders may experience a paradox because they are called to minister for God and enjoy Sabbath rest. Hebrews 4:9-10 provides a resolution, "There remains therefore a Sabbath rest for the people of God. For one who has entered his rest has himself also rested from his works, as God did from his." Does the writer of Hebrews suggest Sabbath rest is only eschatological or can believers enter this rest in their present human condition? The Gospels report that Jesus invited all who were weary to come to him and he would give rest to those who responded obediently (Matt. 11:28). Jesus is the Lord of the Sabbath (Matt. 12:8) and the Alpha and Omega (Rev. 1:8), and he rewards his followers with rest now and in eternity through their obedience.

Believers need rest that extends beyond physical and mental rest and includes refreshment of our spirits. If we understand rest in Hebrews 4 as only eschatological, it may hinder our ability to incorporate spiritual rest into our lives' daily rhythms. Our inability or unwillingness to enter God's spiritual rest may lead to CF. Our embrace of spiritual rest refreshes and rejuvenates us and enhances

> Neglect of Sabbath is sinful disobedience.

77

other forms of physical and emotional rest. Stephen Geller identifies how our understanding of spiritual rest may affect our understanding of rest in Hebrews 4:

> Contemporary distortion [sic] of how human beings live in time are driven by economic, technological, cultural and social forces. It is encouraging to note that scholars and social reformers are beginning to address many aspects of the problem. But the contemporary problem with time is also profoundly spiritual, and it is even more profoundly theological. With a sense of time's importance at this level, it seems unlikely that hard-pressed people will find the strength to resist and restructure dominant patterns.[65]

Geller may be on to something. If we exclude spiritual rest from our personal equation for a balanced life, the contemporary distortions and sensory stimuli that result reduce our ability to address

> Rest is not idleness; it is stress-less productivity.

our overworked physical and emotional needs. Not addressing the spiritual need for rest results in an unbalanced life and incomplete rest. Geller reinforces the need to change our neglect of our spiritual beings and suggests that Sabbath rest involves more than time management:

> Sabbath observance is not meant to be a replacement for time management (which has merit in its place), and it may not even bring balance and personal ful-

fillment. Instead, Sabbath observance fosters a difference that permits faithful people to practice the freedom that is theirs in Christ and to expand their capacity to understand themselves and the world as belonging not to Father Time, with his pocket watch or digital readout, but to God the Creator and Lord of all.[66]

The rest described in Hebrews chapter four is a spiritual rest believers can experience now. In "Reclaimed by Sabbath Rest," Robert Sherman describes this rest as a divine concept that does not reduce Sabbath rest to a time management component and affirms Geller's idea that Sabbath rest governs time:

> Observing the Sabbath affirms that God remains Lord over all time, so that our competing and often conflicting secular understanding of time are [*sic*] shown to be encompassed by a larger, divine purpose and goal. For Christians, practicing Sabbath rest is not a spiritual exercise in a temporal vacuum, but rather an eschatological gift that actually anchors our time.[67]

If we understand rest in Hebrews chapter four as only eschatological, we may neglect the present Sabbath rest available to believers who respond to Jesus Christ's invitation.

Church leaders must minister in their own strength if they do not enter Sabbath rest. Unwillingness to enter Sabbath rest is disobedience, reflects a lack of trust in God's plan, and reveals lack of faith. Lack of faith is sin, "Whatever is not from faith, is sin" (Romans 14:23c), and the Holy Spirit empowers and strengthens church leaders to accomplish God's plan for their lives. God creates an environment of faith and rest, not an environment of stress and faithlessness. Rest is not idleness; it is stress-less productivity.

God does not tire. He does not need a day off or a place to sit so he can catch his breath and wipe his brow. He maintains oversight and care for his creation and is not overwhelmed by his creatures' prayers and requests. In *The Rest of God*, Mark Buchanan describes the difference between the Creator and the created:

> "God is complete without rest. But, not us."

> [God] neither sleeps nor slumbers. He runs no risk of breakdown, burnout, exhaustion, injury. God doesn't need Sabbath or sabbatical. He doesn't pine for vacation. He doesn't require a good night's sleep to clear His head or steady His hand. He doesn't run ragged and run amok, pushing himself beyond his limits, patching Himself together between bursts of striving and binges of workaholism. God is not waiting for the weekend. God is complete without rest. But, not us. For us rest is indispensable.[68]

Jesus subjected himself to the physical and emotional limitations as a human being (Phil. 2:5-8) who required

Sabbath rest for rejuvenation and strength. Jesus led the way for entering into Sabbath rest by taking time to enter the presence of God through prayer and solitude (Mark 1:35). God commands rest in the Old Testament (Exod. 20:8, Deut. 5:12) and invites believers to rest in the New Testament (Matt. 11:28).

Rest for church leaders is more than relief of weariness, and it is not just a day off or a time of study. Rather, this rest involves leaders' complete lives. In *The Sabbath: Its Meaning for Modern Man*, Abraham Herschel writes:

> Sabbath rest is spiritual and not something we accomplish. Rest is a place we enter.

> The Sabbath is a day for the sake of life. Man is not a beast of burden and the Sabbath is not for the purpose of enhancing the efficiency of his work. . . . The Sabbath is not for the sake of the weekdays: the weekdays are for the sake of the Sabbath. It is not an interlude, but the climax of living.[69]

Church leaders' struggle to take Sabbath rest may result from the notion at the end of the day that they have accomplished little or nothing. One day may seem to flow into the next, days into weeks, and weeks into months with little progress. Church leaders may believe their work is never being done, and they ask: "If I never complete six days of work, how can I rest?" Barbara Brown Taylor writes in "Sabbath Resistance," "One day each week I live as if all my work were done."[70] Church leaders can apply this concept and rest from the perpetual demands of ministry. In so doing, they acknowledge that rest after the sixth working day is God's plan for health and longevity in ministry.

Moses: An Early Church Leader

Moses felt considerable stress when God called him to lead Israel out of captivity and into the Promise Land. Nearly two million people had been captive slaves without a day off for four hundred years. Moses killed an Egyptian because the Egyptian mistreated his people (Exod. 2:11-15). Years later, things went from bad to worse when Moses approached Pharaoh and asked him to free the Israelites. The slaves were forced to do more with less while Moses negotiated their freedom, and the Israelites became angry and frustrated because of the added burden Pharaoh put on them. They expressed their emotions to Moses before their release from Egypt and again at the edge of the Red Sea as Pharaoh's army pursued them.

They grumbled and complained while safe and secure on the other side of the sea. They lacked food, but when God supplied manna, the Israelites considered it boring and mundane. Water was scarce. God supplied water at the pond at Marah, but the water was bitter. Moses' unhappy followers became as bitter as the water, and they focused their anger on Moses.

The stress of leading took its toll on Moses. During a great battle, Aaron and Hur held up Moses' arms to assure victory, but the pressure on Moses did not ease up after the battle. Moses' father-in-law saw the stress Moses experienced and told Moses, "The thing that you are doing is not good. You will surely wear out, both yourself and these people who are with you, for the task is too heavy for you; you cannot do it alone" (Exod. 18:17-18). This wisdom survives, and many leadership seminars and seminary courses emphasize leaders' limitations and the need to delegate. This is a simple Old Testament truth that helps church leaders avoid CF.

> The stress of leading took its toll on Moses.

God's workers are called to undershepherd their flocks and rest in Christ. Sabbath rest is spiritual and not something they accomplish. Rest is a place they enter, a place made for them by Christ's completed work on the cross. Church leaders draw strength from the Good Shepherd (John 10:10) as King David wrote long ago, "The Lord is my shepherd, I shall not want. He makes me lie down in green pastures; he leads me by the still waters. He restores my soul" (Ps. 23:1-3a).

Sabbath neglect reflects a lack of faith. The writer of Hebrews states, "Let us, therefore, be diligent to enter that same rest, lest anyone fall through following the same example of disobedience" (Heb. 4:11). Hebrews 4 declares that God created Sabbath rest and desires to meet his followers, but many followers are too busy doing work God already completed to enter into his presence.

Sabbath rest is more than a day off, an annual vacation, or a life separated from the world. This is especially true if we feel guilty about not doing something, or doing things that were not completed in the other six days. My seminary colleague, John Stumbo, described what Sabbath rest meant to him, "Hearing God's permission to accomplish nothing"[71] that allows God to accomplish something new in your life. Wayne Muller describes what God expects from us during our Sabbath observance:

Sabbath requires surrender. If we only stop when we are finished with all our work, we will never stop-because our work is never completely done. With every accomplishment there arises a new responsibility. Every swept floor invites another sweeping, every child bathed invites another bathing. When all life moves in such cycles, what is ever finished? If we refuse rest until we are finished, we will never rest until we die. Sabbath dissolves the artificial urgency of our days, *because it liberates us from the need to be finished.*[72]

Eugene Peterson wrote *Working the Angles* and describes a day off as a "bastard Sabbath."[73] A day off has benefits, but it is not a Sabbath. Peterson suggests the motive for a day off is as a source of more productivity on the other six days. This is an incorrect motive for rest, and Peterson writes, "Mental and physical health improves markedly with a day off. . . . The motivation is utilitarian: the day off is at the service of the six working days."[74] My Christmas Day Sabbath may fit Peterson's category of non-Sabbath time off.

The biblical concept of Sabbath may be extreme in our church culture. Leaders are expected to be busy interacting with non-Christians, counseling, visiting the sick and lonely, and training believers in leadership, missions, evangelism, and biblical doctrine.

> The offspring of willingness and obedience is the favor of God.

Barbara Brown Taylor described her feelings, "If I stopped for a whole day, God would be sorely disappointed in me."[75] Her statement may reflect a lack of faith in God's call on church leaders' lives. God wants obedience, not performance. God calls church leaders to obedience that includes Sabbath rest.

A missionary shared how God gave him ministry opportunities among people of great importance and wealth. He said this was not because of his skills or wisdom. In fact these people considered him too young to possess wisdom. Instead he said, "The offspring of willingness and obedience is the favor of God."[77] He found God's favor through obedience and following God's call.

The same holds true for Sabbath rest. We must obey the fourth commandment willingly and experience Sabbath rest as part of our lives' healthy rhythms. Compassion fatigue is the opposite of obedience, willingness, and Sabbath observance. Our cessation of ministry busyness and our entry into rest and God's presence provides re-creation, refreshment, peace, and abundant life.

Observing Sabbath

"Freedom 55" is an insurance company ad that promises we will reach age 55, stop work, and enjoy our retirement dreams through proper investments. These are retirement dreams because we must work long hours, many overtime shifts, and save for this future "rest and re-creation." Mary Lou Weisman writes in the New York Times:

> Even in biblical times, when a fair number of people made it into old age, retirement still had not been invented and respect for old people remained high. In those days, it was customary to carry on until you dropped, regardless of your age group—no shuffleboard, no Airstream trailer. When a patriarch could no longer farm, herd cattle or pitch a tent, he opted for more specialized, less labor-intensive work, like prophesying and handing down commandments. Or he moved in with his kids.[77]

Retirement has existed for only about the last one hundred years and only in wealthy nations, but it shapes our work ethic and changes how we live. The retirement dream and hope for secure finances on our fifty-fifth birthday affects church leaders' lives. There is nothing wrong with retiring, but failure to

> Retirement has existed for only about the last one hundred years.

follow God's prescription for rest is wrong. Rest is a rhythm of life, not a reward for wise financial planning.

God planned that our lifetimes must include *shabbat* or Sabbath rest. Life is a cycle of work and rest, not work, work, work, and then rest. God did not plan that his creatures labor for years without rest and then cease work and enter into eternal rest. The Creator gives directions for life for his creation, including those called to lead his church.

The concept of rest assumed new meaning in the New Testament. Jesus reintroduced rest's importance when he said, "Come unto me, all who are weary and heaven laden and I will give you rest . . . and you will find rest for your souls." (Matt. 11:28-9). Rest was no longer a directive, but the embodiment of God in Jesus Christ. Rest was no longer on a "do and don't" list for Jehovah's followers, but a person who gave believers his rest.

The neglect of Sabbath causes compassion fatigue and other related stressors among pastors and church leaders, and may trigger an inability to follow God's call. The pressures of success, materialism, job security, and poor time management replace the gentle peace and rest the Lord's presence offers. In *Jesus on Leadership*, C. Gene Wilkes asserts, "The differences between those who lead out of their natural motives and those who lead from a spiritual base are clear. Jesus modeled the power of authentic, spiritual leadership."[78] The opposite often occurs in North American church culture.

James and John went to the temple after Pentecost and told the crippled man at the temple that they were poor, "Silver and gold have I none." (Acts 3:6). Instead they proclaimed power in Christ's name, pulled the man to his feet, and he ran into the temple completely healed. The North American church has silver and gold but may lack Christ's power. Building size, the number of campuses, the number of pastoral staff and media fame are not biblical success standards.

> The North American church has silver and gold but lacks Christ's power.

Today's Sabbath Observance

North American churches neglect the fourth commandment and its New Testament counterpart. Leaders busy themselves with "God things." They mentor congregations of busy people involved in families, careers, eldercare, and the accumulation of money for early retirement and rest.

People may someday seek rest and time, rather than money or possessions, becoming the most sought after currency for mankind. Time is in short supply and lack of time creates lack of rest. The need for rest and peace is not a new phenomenon, and Annie Payson Call describes the condition of American culture at the turn of the nineteenth century:

Nervous disorders, resulting from over-work are all about us. Extreme nervous tension seems to be so peculiarly American, that a German physician coming to this country to practice became puzzled by the variety of nervous disorders he was called upon to help and finally announced his discovery of a new disease which he chose to call, "Americanitis." And now we suffer from "Americanitis" in all its unlimited varieties.[79]

> Materialism became a worship object.

Leigh Eric Schmidt describes Annie Call's mission in *Restless Souls*:

Call wanted to compose and relax Americans, to heal them of their enervating worries and fears, through "mind training" or "true concentration." Her program was premised on a quieting of the body and mind— release of contracted muscles, the counting of slow breaths, the elimination of distracting thought.[80]

The church was once the authoritative on social or spiritual knowledge, and the church steeple stood higher than any other community structure. This changed as other spiritual groups offered answers for peace and rest to restless people involved in the dynamic North American culture. For example, Annie Besant advocates "Thought Power" to eradicate worry, "Let, then, a person, who is suffering from worry, give three or four minutes in the morning, on first rising, to some noble and encouraging thought, 'The Self is Peace; that Self is Strength; that Self am I.'"[81]

Schmidt describes these alternate teachings, "Across the board, meditation was heralded as a salve for anxiety and as an unrivaled source of serenity."[82] The North American culture spins out of control through busyness and stress, and anxiety and lack of peace combine negatively with a shortage of time. As a result, many embrace non-biblical alternatives or experience out of control lives.

The Object of Worship Has Changed

Societal changes since WWII also transformed church culture, and materialism became a worship object. Webster defines worship as "extravagant respect or admiration for or devotion to an object of esteem (*worship* of the dollar)."[83] North American culture evolved into a must have environment with busy people driven by self-gratification and an insatiable appetite for the newest gadget. Consequently, they spend less time at rest in the Creator's presence, neglect Sabbath, and suffer as a result. Schaller reinforces this thought, and he describes the loss of rural life:

> The combination of the erosion of inherited institutional loyalties, the widespread ownership of the private motor vehicle, good roads, the growth of individualism, the increased geographical separation of the place of work from the place of residence, and the growing competition for the loyalty of the consumer has transformed American society.[84]

The deconstruction of Sabbath observance led people to explore mysticism offered by meditation and inner peace evangelists. The church offered peace and rest only in words, and its leaders fell victim to stress that was far from peace and rest.

Pastors and church leaders populate the frontline of the rat race. These ministers, like Moses, know the fourth commandment God etched on granite with his own finger and his instructions about healthy and productive living. Like Moses, however, they often fail to observe God's prescription for rest. Eugene Peterson argues:

The dogma (we practice a theology that puts moral effort as the primary element in pleasing God) produces the behavior characteristics of the North American pastor. If things are not good enough, they will improve if we work a little harder and get others to work harder. Add a committee, here recruit some volunteers there, and squeeze a couple of more hours into the workday.[85]

Peterson believes the Sabbath-keeping commandment is broken most often and without remorse:

No other commandment is treated with such disregard as this one. . . . Perhaps that is why the Sabbath is *commanded* not *suggested,* for nothing less than a command has the power to intervene in the vicious, accelerating, self-perpetuating cycle of faithless and graceless busyness, the only part of which we are conscious being our good intentions.[86]

Some congregants believe pastors work only on Sunday morning, and this perception causes some pastors to prove the opposite is true. Gary Preston writes about a pastor's battle to please the masses, "Pastors often follow an unwritten law that says we have to put in enough hours so that no one will ever doubt our commitment to sacrificial ministry. The last thing most of us want to hear is, 'I don't think you're working hard enough, Pastor.'"[87]

Often weddings or funerals happen on pastors' personal Sabbath days. They may take another day off, but it often becomes another day of ministry. Pagers and cell phones are barriers to pastoral Sabbaths that keep pastors connected on days off or at retreats, and they may be summoned at a moment's notice. Cell phones are technological shackles and keep central nervous systems on constant alert. It is impossible for pastors' bodies and minds to rest and experience Sabbath as God intended.

God planned for us to work, "Six days shall you labor and do all your work" (Exod. 20:9), but he also planned rest, "[B]ut, the seventh day is the Sabbath of the Lord your God, in it you shall not do any work" (Exod. 20:10). God established laws through the Decalogue, and disobedience of God's word is a sin that separates us from God. Jesus is our salvation; we receive his gift of forgiveness, are reconciled with God, and enter God's presence when we fellowship with him as did Adam and Eve. Jesus enhances our relationship through rest in his presence, and he invites those who are weary. Why do church leaders and pastors neglect such an important gift from God? It may be as a result of our attempt to meet our needs in our own ways, and it will lead to compassion fatigue.

Shabbat
Relax and Re-Create

When was the last time you took time off and accomplished nothing? Did you feel guilty?

A missionary said, "The offspring of willingness and obedience is the favor of God." Are you in his favor?

Graph your rhythms of life. Have you included sufficient rest times in the cycle?

What would happen if you stopped for a day? a week? a month?

What are you modeling for your staff? (Work hard? Always be available?)

What is your idea of retirement? Do you have a retirement plan?

Read Mark Buchanan, **The Rest of God** *(Nashville, TN: W Publishing Group, 2006).*

CHAPTER FOUR

LEADERSHIP

Follow my example, as I follow the example of Christ.
The Apostle Paul,
(1 Corinthians 11:1 NIV)

The Canadian Broadcasting Company interviewed a young medical student about his decision to become a physician.[88] The interviewer asked whether he would choose family medicine or a specialty such as emergency medicine. He said he would choose a specialty. His father was family physician in a small town, and he acknowledged his father's job satisfaction; however, he saw the toll it took on personal and family life. A specialty like emergency medicine provided a higher income and greater status. The interviewer reported that young physicians differ from their

> They want lives beyond their jobs.

workaholic fathers. They want lives beyond their jobs. They prefer to work forty to forty-five hours a week and spend more time with their families. The interviewer added, "The upshot is that a family doctor trained in 2007 will be about seventy to seventy five percent as 'productive' as a doctor who was trained in the 1980s." The church faces a similar problem. Seminary graduates are more likely to choose a specialized ministry such as youth ministry or assistant pastorate, rather than a senior pastor position. The reasons are echoed in the interviewer's comments, "They want a life beyond their job."[90]

The church leadership crisis is not as public as the family physician shortage, but it also affects society. Filling senior pastoral positions is a serious problem and will worsen if church leadership paradigms don't shift. Many young seminary graduates choose specialized ministries and avoid the vacant offices of senior pastors. The image of overworked pastors, who would be considered the spiritual family physicians of previous decades, is unattractive to this new breed of church leaders. Instead, these young people consider what is important to them and their future in ministry. This new concept of leadership is not necessarily wrong, but it will change how the church operates in the future.

My question is, "What will this new paradigm look like and how will it affect the church in our postmodern society?" This chapter provides a biblical view of leadership, discusses present day church leadership styles, and suggests a paradigm shift needed for vital, relevant, balanced ministry in the coming decades that reduces the risk of CF.

The Evolution of Leadership

The church has evolved through the centuries and a part of that evolution was significant changes in leadership styles and duties. The leaders Jesus chose to perpetuate his church differed from the religious leaders of his time, and church leadership has been in flux since Christ's ascension. The contemporary church faces a serious challenge to its traditional hierarchal leadership structure, which was the accepted model for centuries. Many church leaders in our culture admit the

> Many nights the shepherd remained awake, oversaw his flock, protected them from possible attack, and developed strategies to feed and water them the next day.

need for change so that they can reach our North American culture more effectively. This change is happening.

What will leadership look like for those currently in church leadership positions? Will this change resemble an Old Testament leadership model or embrace the New Testament leader/disciple pattern? Will it reestablish Constantine's hierarchal form of leadership with popes, elders, and CEOs or will servants lead from within the crowd? What are the risk factors involved in these differing leadership models?

The Shepherd School

Leadership began with God who gave humanity dominion over the earth. God called Adam to exercise dominion over the animals, and He named them as the first leader within the creation. Adam was in charge of all of God's earthly creation. God knew Adam was unable to accomplish this feat by himself and so He created Eve, "a helper suitable for him" (Genesis 2:18). After God created Eve, God called Adam and Eve to populate the earth and tend the garden. This act of creating Eve to work alongside of Adam indicates God's desire for team ministry. From the beginning, God's plan for leadership included a team to share the responsibility and the workload. Moses was such a leader.

God summoned Moses to Egypt, and he led thousands from bondage into freedom. This freedom walk demanded every bit of character, virtue, and leadership skill Moses possessed. God equipped Moses with the necessary skills in anticipation of the task. In *Shepherds after My Own Heart,* Timothy S. Laniak stresses that the forty years in the "School of Desert Shepherding" developed Moses' leadership skills for Israel's deliverance from Egyptian bondage. Laniak writes, "It would be better to say that Moses was, *as a shepherd,* a prophetic miracle worker, covenant mediator, military leader, priestly intercessor and source of divine direction and provision. He was the human instrument by which God comprehensively shepherded his flock."[91]

Laniak describes the desert environment's importance in Moses' character and skill development. For example, many nights the shepherd remained awake, oversaw his flock, protected them from possible attack, and developed strategies to feed and water them the next day. In the safety of the morning the shepherd called his sheep, and they responded to his voice. They began the journey to a new location and completely trusted the shepherd's skills.

Laniak describes the significance of the shepherding experience for Moses and believes it was the best schooling a leader could receive, "This occupation put shepherds in a constant state of negotiation with an unpredictable physical and social environment. For these and other reasons, the shepherd naturally became an icon of leadership."[92]

Early in his leadership, Moses found himself at war. The physical and emotional cost he experienced as he led his people through battle drained him. For example, Moses began to tire during the battle between Amalek and Israel. When He was able to hold his hand high towards the Lord, Israel became victorious. When his hand dropped, Amalek became victorious. The fatigue could have cost Israel the victory, but it was overcome when two of Moses' leadership team placed him in a position of rest (sitting on a rock) and held his arms up (Exodus 17:8-13). This support from Aaron and Hur allowed Moses to lead Israel on to victory. The emotional and physical cost of spiritual warfare for church leaders can result in CF. Allowing others to lift up your arms and placing yourself in a position of rest may help leaders avoid the debilitating effects of CF.

Larger flocks require more shepherds. Moses tried to care for the people completely by himself until Jethro, an experienced shepherd, intervened and shared the principal of delegation. Moses learned quickly that leadership is often more than one person can handle adequately. Jethro suggested Moses delegate some of the leadership tasks to others. Under Jethro's direction, Moses selected capable, trustworthy leaders who feared the Lord and did not seek dishonest gain. He placed them over thousands, hundreds, fifties, and tens, and empowered them to settle simple everyday situations (Exodus 18).

Immediately following the victory over the Amalekites and the instruction from Jethro regarding organization of his new staff of conflict resolution specialists, Moses encountered God on Mount Sinai. These events all took place in a period of less than three months. Moses received God's most significant directive concerning stress management in leadership. God prescribed balance for Moses' life and for the nation of Israel. God spoke of a relationship between God and humans (Exodus 20:1-7), of relationships among individual humans (Exodus 20:12-17), the avoidance of sin against one another, self-care, and the need for rest (Exodus 20:8-11). God mentored Moses' personally in the area of balanced leadership. A healthy life within God's parameters can reduce stressors and the risk of CF.

A couple of years ago I attended a seminar for pastors and church leaders. The evening speaker talked about longevity in the ministry, and said he became the "medicine man" after two and a half decades leading the same church. He used the medicine man metaphor and indicated that after pastoring the flock for this period of time, he established his leadership and won the trust of his team and flock. During his steadfast life and ministry, this pastor proved that God had anointed him and congregants believed God called him as their shepherd. In *Sociology of Religion,* Joachim Wach describes the influence priests and magicians (medicine men) have in their caring positions:

> It is frequently difficult to differentiate properly between the magician and the priest. The former forces the deity or the spirits to obey him; the latter submits his will to the divine. Though the popular authority of the priest derives mostly from those activities which distribute the blessings of the gods to the individuals and groups, it rests ultimately on his communion with the numen expressed in formalized cult. Because the numen is attended, there is the expectation that the special desires of the people may be fulfilled by the deity.[93]

Moses was the medicine man through whom God established priestly care giving ministry. Moses received instructions from God (the numen) to ordain Aaron and his sons to maintain the perpetual flame of the tabernacle lamp (Exodus

27:20-21). This narrative describes God's call, anointing, and commissioning of Aaron and his sons for the spiritual care of the Israelites. God established ritual, consecration, and protocol for the care of Israel administered by the Levites, a tribe of spiritual caregivers. Moses' brother, Aaron, led the tribe; however, his leadership faltered. Moses went up the mountain and met with God a second time and, in his absence, the nation of Israel became corrupt. Anxiety and fear filled those who waited for Moses' return. Stress overcame Aaron and he engaged in the sin of idolatry (Exodus 32:19-24). Instead of resting in the presence of God until Moses returned, Aaron engaged in ungodly behavior. The last discourse God between Moses before his descent was the discussion of the value of Sabbath observance (Exodus 31:12-18).

Human fallibility surfaces when lack of faith disturbs the spiritual connection with God. Fear and anxiety undermine believers' faith and may lead to temptation. When believers yield to temptation, it results in sin and death. James writes, "But each one is tempted when he is carried away and enticed by his own lust. Then when lust has conceived, it gives birth to sin; and when sin is accomplished, it brings forth death" (James 1:14-15).

Chapter Two of this book identified the susceptibility of leaders who self-medicate to numb pain and find relief when stressed or depleted of compassion and emotional reserve. Instead of practicing Shabbat and finding divine rest, peace, healing, and strengthening their faith, the Israelites found themselves in the jaws of the devouring lion described in 1 Peter 5:6-10.

Eventually, God transferred the spiritual leadership in the Old Testament from the priests to the prophets. The priesthood contaminated the sacred offering through corruption, sexual sin, and complacency (1 Samuel 1:12-17, 22-26). God raised up Samuel and other prophets who replaced the contaminated priests. This replacement refocused Israelites on the holiness of God and the Decalogue.

Stress affected the priesthood, judges, prophets, and kings. When stress affects leaders it empties their hearts of compassion, and they may become complacent about the things of God. Weakness may lead them to temptation, self-medication, and sin that separate them from God. Leaders should be conscious of factors that lead to physical, mental, or spiritual weakness. All caregivers should understand God's prescription for health, longevity, balance, holiness, obedience, and Sabbath observance.

Jesus' Leadership Style

> I heard her calling, "Here sheep, here sheep!" They didn't even look up.

The Old Testament writers recognize King David as a great shepherd and described his shepherd leadership model in Psalm 23. The Old Testament shepherd metaphor appears in the New Testament and Jesus' leadership style.

The shepherd metaphor applies to the person of Jesus Christ who called himself the Good Shepherd. He said the good shepherd lays down his life for his sheep, whereas the bad shepherd flees from danger and leaves his sheep vulnerable to the predator's attack. The good shepherd knows his sheep, and they know his voice (John 10:11-15).

The idea that sheep know their shepherd's voice intrigued me, and I experienced this phenomenon. I pastored a church on Saltspring Island early in my ministry, and we lived on a seven-acre farm

> Everyone is important, not only those who are recognized for what they contribute.

and raised sheep. We bought sheep at the local auction and other shepherds gave us old ewes or orphaned lambs. Our flock of seven ewes and fourteen lambs grazed in the field. I approached the gate and called, "Here sheep, here sheep!" and they immediately mobbed me as I went into the field.

One morning my wife went the field and called the sheep. She carried a bundle of corn stalks and cobs that the sheep loved. She called, "Here sheep, here sheep!" They didn't even look up. She changed her voice and tried to sound like me, but that didn't work either. She rustled the corn stalks to focus attention on their favorite meal, and they ignored her. I walked down to the gate and called the sheep, "Here sheep, here sheep!" and they ran past her and surrounded me. Sheep know their shepherd's voice.

Jesus said the sheep know his voice, and voice recognition depends on hearing, responding to, and reinforcing what is heard. Jesus was close to those he led, they were familiar with him, and they knew he cared for them. Charles C. Manz in his introduction to *The Leadership Wisdom of Jesus,* describes Jesus' personal connections and relational leadership style. Manz describes the encouragement this strategy created in Jesus' followers:

> I believe that all human beings desire (and perhaps require), at some level, dignity and commitment to a positive spiritual connection with others. Treating people right and helping them to be right with themselves and the rest of the world is perhaps the only legitimate choice for long-term effective leadership.[94]

In his parables about the lost sheep and the lost coin, Jesus made the point that everyone is important, not only those who are recognized for what they contribute. You are valuable in Jesus' eyes just because you are who you are.

Walter C. Wright reinforces the idea of relational style leading in his book, *Relational Leadership*. He writes about an influential young priest who moved to a small First Nations village in the interior of British Columbia and died three years later from cancer. In his three-year journey, this young priest did more than offer the ministry of his office or church position. He also led through relationship and taught the villagers about God's love, living life, and Christ's death.

Wright says, "If by *leader* we mean a person who enters into a relationship with another person to influence their [*sic*] behavior, values, and attitudes, then I would suggest that all Christians should be leaders. Or, perhaps more accurately, all Christians should exercise leadership, attempting to make a difference in the lives of those around them."[95] Jesus made a difference in the lives of those around him, and those he influenced made a difference in others' lives.

Relational leadership entails vulnerability and comes at a cost. Frank

> "What is to give light must endure burning."

Ochberg explains this reality, "Every person who moves towards the person in pain to help, everyone who comforts someone who is in pain, everyone who listens closely with sensitivity, is a potential casualty."[96] Viktor Frankl quotes Anton Wildgans in *Doctor and the Soul* about the cost of care-giving, "What is to give light must endure burning."[97] The author's wise words remind church leaders of their vulnerability to CF.

Servant leadership is costly. As John records, "Jesus saw that in their enthusiasm, they were about to grab him and make him king, so he slipped off and went back up the mountain to be by himself (John 6:15, *The Message*). Prior to the crowd's invitation, Jesus healed the lame man, learned his cousin John the Baptist was beheaded, was challenged about healing on the Sabbath, received a death threat from religious people, preached to the crowds, and fed 5,000. Jesus was spent emotionally. Now the crowd wanted to make him king. Jesus experienced CF, and John says, "He went back up the mountain to be by himself."

I don't believe that church leaders must die for the church: Christ did that. Nor do I belittle the power of martyrdom for the gospel. I do believe, however, that if Sabbath disobedience or the lack of self-care leads to a church leader's death or failure that death or failure is not laid down for Christ's message. It is death or failure by disobedience or self-neglect.

The servant leadership model does not focus on an organization's bottom line, but on its leaders and followers as valued resources. Manz writes, "To true leaders, every person they lead is priceless. No other organizational resource is of greater value."[98] Jesus empowered his followers through his leadership style. The writer of Luke describes how Jesus sent the seventy to minister (Luke 10) as a training experience that prepared them for church leadership after Pentecost (Acts 1-2).

Jesus Was Not a CEO

Almost every seminar or seminary course emphasizes leadership and leadership skills. This emphasis occurs in the secular world and the church, and strong leadership is essential in our world. The church needs Holy Spirit-directed leadership and the secular world needs more Holy Spirit-filled leaders in companies and institutions. I ask, "How does Jesus' leadership style differ from leadership models used in twenty-first century churches?" Many church leadership models are modified corporate hierarchal structures reworked to fit the church. The gospel accounts of Jesus' leadership present him as a shepherd-facilitator who equipped his team as a servant rather than as the CEO of the New Testament church.

In the corporate world, someone controls and directs an organization's functions. The church is different. Jesus is the head and the church is his body, but he acts as a servant, not as the controlling head of a hierarchical structure. The apostle Paul in his letter to the Philippians describes how Jesus being fully God, humbled himself, "emptied Himself, taking on the form of a bondservant." (Philippians 2:5-8). He is the head of the body, but he serves those who serve.

Leaderless Organizations

Ori Brafman and Rod Beckstrom identify the difference between two types of organizations in their book *The Starfish and the Spider*. The spider-like organization has an essential head, and the organization will collapse and die without the

> The spider-like organization has an essential head. The organization will collapse and die without the direct influence of the head.

head's direct influence. The spider metaphor describes a CEO-led organization in which leadership comes from a key person who holds all the organizational power. This organizational type is common among modern businesses and institutions.

The starfish-like organization's power is not centered in one person; rather its power is distributed among those who adopt the founder's vision. Starfish reproduce themselves if they lose a leg; they do not depend on a head to direct action. The starfish concept of leadership is difficult for modern thinkers to grasp and assimilate in large organizations because they are structured like spiders.

An example in Brafman and Beckstrom's book is Dave Garrison who explained the early Internet to a group of French businessmen interested in investing in his Internet service provider. They did not understand the concept of a leaderless Internet:

> Under the pressure, Garrison told the investors that he was the president of the Internet.

> Dave recalls that their questions were "based on the concept of 'it has to be centralized, there has to be a king, or there has to be an emperor, or there has to be a something.'" These key investors—"probably thirty

people in a room in one of the five star hotels," Dave recalls—were a "very intelligent group of people," but they didn't get it. Dave tried another approach: the Internet was a network of networks. "We said, 'There are thirty to forty thousand networks, and all share the burden of communication.' And they said, "But who decides?" And we said, "No one decides. It's a standard that people subscribe to. No one decides." And they kept coming back, saying, "You don't understand the question, it must be lost in the translation, who is the president of the Internet?"[99]

Under the pressure, Garrison told the investors that he was the president. The investors now had their hierarchal structure and could continue discussions.

Do contemporary church members believe a CEO is essential? Has the church missed the Holy Spirit's message about the diversity of gifts and callings in the body of Christ? Can the body function without a visible, tangible head? Christ practiced a hybrid model of leadership that demonstrates the head need not be the center of power and authority. People attributed authority to Jesus through his servant leadership as the writer of Philippians explains, "Who, being in the form of God, thought it not robbery to be equal with God: But made himself of no repu-

tation, and took upon him the form of a servant and was made in

> Jesus is the ultimate "hybrid leader."

the likeness of men." (Philippians 2:6-7, KJV). Jesus led without the need to be recognized as the leader.

The metaphor of an organization as a starfish or a spider helps analyze the church's condition in the twenty-first century. Brafman and Beckstrom offer a hybrid spider/starfish model as a third option and use eBay as an example:

> Up to this point, we've looked at companies at one end of the centralization continuum or the other: eBay represents the combo special. It's neither a pure starfish nor a pure spider, but what we call a hybrid organization. Companies like eBay combine the best of both worlds—the bottom up approach of decentralization and the structure, control, and resulting profit potential of centralization. Representing the first of two types of hybrid organizations, eBay is *a centralized company that decentralizes the customer experience.*[100]

Internet companies such as eBay and amazon.com have corporate headquarters, but they also benefit from site users' input. Customer networking generates much of the traffic for these companies. Customers develop trust and become "owners" with input through, for example, posting reviews.

Jesus came and established his church. He chose and invested in twelve team members, equipped them, and charged them to take his message and church worldwide.

Jesus remains the head, but he decentralized power and gave believers supernatural gifts to disseminate the gospel message in every language. He is the head, but he delegates the Kingdom's business to his body on earth. He is the head, but the church is his body in action. He trusts the church and asks only that believers communicate with him regularly through prayer and refer to Bible for directions. This system has worked well and grown continuously for two thousand years. When church leaders work together in this

> From all accounts it appears Jesus put together a very messy team.

context with Christ, the reliance for strength and refreshing comes through him. When a church leader neglects his or her rest, the result is often CF.

Team Building by Jesus

Did Jesus follow the proper steps in choosing his team members? Did he check their personality profiles against other team members to see if they fit? Did he hold a weekend retreat where profiles identified their personality types, leadership skills, and expertise? Were the team members given written job descriptions and a benefit plan? Were they on probation for the first six months and, following a satisfactory evaluation, re-evaluated every six months? How were promotions given? Could they expect to move up the leadership ladder based on performance? Who led the group? Who managed the retreat? Who facilitated the discussion?

From the gospel accounts it appears Jesus put together a very messy team. The disciples' Myers-Brigs Personality profiles[101] might show many combinations of extroversion/introversion, sensing/intuition, feeling/thinking, and judging/perceiving. The results of their criminal record checks might raise red flags. When you add life skills and former careers to this mix, it is easy to see that Jesus did not surround himself with people who would make him look good. His team was eclectic, diverse, and imperfect.

Jesus' selected disciples based on a prayerful process. He knew the hearts of his followers, accepted them at face value, mentored them, and built a team that multiplied into other teams. He knew the church would survive until his return.

Most twenty-first century team-building seminars and books omit the components of Jesus' "messy" team; however, Eric Abrahamson and David Freedman describe the hidden benefits of disorder in *A Perfect Mess*. They believe one of the strengths of mess is its robustness, which describes the disciples, "Robustness: Because mess tends to loosely weave together disparate elements, messy systems are more resistant to destruction, failure and imitation. Neat systems tend to have more sharply defined strong and weak points, and thus are often brittle, easily foiled or disrupted, and easily copied."[102]

In *Courageous Leadership,* Bill Hybels discusses building a kingdom dream team and describes the "Three Cs" he uses to choose his team members, "Character, Competence, and Chemistry." Hybels says they are the winning ingredients for building a dream team. Hybels writes about competence:

> If I am looking for a Director of Operations, I look for someone with a monster administrative gift and a stellar track record of performance. Years ago I realized that if I didn't start surrounding myself with some really outstanding people I would be overwhelmed by the challenges of leading Willow. Now when I look around the table during our management team meetings I see a Harvard MBA, a Stanford MBA, one PhD, two individuals with law degrees and several with master's degrees. I am the only one seriously lacking in credentials![103]

Jesus did the opposite. When he built his team he called a tax collector, who might be considered a MBA equivalent, but Jesus did not give him the job of looking after the books. He chose a team member who was dishonest and skimmed from the moneybag. Jesus did not surround himself with outstanding people; he surrounded himself with people, gave them opportunity to become outstanding, and poured himself into their lives.

Servant Leadership

Many churches today are operated like a business, but usual business models do not reflect the church's God-given purpose. Jesus commissioned his followers to, "go forth and make disciples of all nations" (Matthew 28:19). Jesus alluded to a paradigm shift in human life when he spoke to his followers about pouring new wine into new wine skins (Mark 2). Jesus used this imagery and taught his disciples that a complete change, a complete newness, must take place on the inside and outside. Otherwise, the old garment or vessels, which are metaphors for persons called by God, cannot adjust to the changes, and disaster results.

Mark records Jesus' two metaphors that describe change. The first was that of a new cloth patch sewn on old clothing; the patch tears away when someone washes the old garment. The second was pouring new wine into old wine skins. The old wine skin cannot withstand the action of the new wine, and the old wineskin explodes. Change suggests newness, and newness is essential to how church leaders live lead. The church is a living and breathing organism, living organisms change, and the church should change constantly. Christian Swartz talks about this natural growth process in *Natural Church Development*. He believes the church grows in a healthy manner through the biotic process, which "ecologists [describe] as 'the inherent capacity of an organism or species to reproduce and survive.'"[104] This healthy growth produces healthy change. C. Gene Wilkes believes, "'Jesus' entire ministry was about service to his Father in heaven, service to his mission, service to his followers and ultimately, service to those he came to save."[105] Jesus is the servant leader, and his life and leadership style form the pattern for church leaders. Contemporary church leaders should revisit his model of servant leadership. Jesus modeled authenticity in His leadership, leading with all authority, but with the heart of a servant.

Authentic Leadership

I believe the contemporary body of Christ hungers for an authentic Spirit-led servant leadership. I use the word "body" instead of "church" intentionally. Contemporary use of the word "church" may connote a building or a hierarchal organization that operates in a mechanical or liturgical manner. Rejection of this model seems especially prevalent in the postmodern community as Kenneth Boa describes in *The Perfect Leader.* He writes, "People are not impressed by facades or manipulation, but by authenticity and by those who are genuinely others-centered. Character is not a matter of outward technique, but of inner reality."[106]

Boa describes the North American postmodern generation. He suggests that people do not seek a religion to join; instead they seek real, authentic relationships with the living God. He believes effective leadership in Christ's body mimics Jesus and allows his presence and compassion to fuel leadership opportunities. It does not mimic the culture and its successful leaders. Boa writes, "True spiritual and character transformation takes place from the inside out, not from the outside in. The attributes of faith, goodness, knowledge, self-control, perseverance, godliness, brotherly kindness, and love flow from the life of Christ that has been implanted in us."[107]

Carly Fiorina describes a leader's character in *Tough Choices*. She writes about values instilled in her as a child: success was not fame and fortune, but the quality of one's mind and character:

> Character was everything, and character was defined as candor, integrity and authenticity. Candor was about speaking the truth and about speaking up and speaking out. Integrity was about preserving your principles and acting on them. Authenticity was about knowing what you believed, being who you were, and standing up for both.[108]

Boa and Fiorina believe leaders' success lies in character. I believe character can reflect God, and God calls leaders to be servants rather than self-serving CEOs. God ordains all Christians to lead as followers of Jesus, regardless of position inside or outside the church. A freshness of the Holy Spirit's power and anointing on church leaders causes them to yearn for an encounter with God. We will explore this aspect in the following chapter.

Mentoring Leadership

Leaders have followers. Followers need mentoring, and mentoring is a leadership skill often emphasized in leadership seminars. Jesus mentored effectively. The disciples lived, ate, and slept with him. They saw every aspect of his life. He taught compassion through his emotional expression at Lazarus' death (John 11:32), how to believe in miracles when he raised Lazarus from the dead (John 11:38), how to care for others when he fed the

> Jesus taught his team how to serve others.

multitudes (Matthew 14), and how to pray (Matthew 6). Jesus demonstrated his power over evil when he cast out demons (Matthew 8:32).

Many contemporary CEOs delegate mentoring to expert consultants. In twenty-first century churches and secular organizations, many CEOs fail to mentor even their closest team members. Jesus taught his team how to serve others. The gospels share no accounts of Jesus teaching about church growth, but he did mentor his followers. They believed his message, followed him, and became disciples. Jesus taught the value of life that all persons are created in the image of God, and all have value, worth, and purpose. In *Servant*

Leadership, Robert Greenleaf admits his non-theological view of religion; however, he cites the power of mentoring others as a servant leader:

> What made George Fox's service to seekers (and their response to him) so exemplary was the significant move to new and more exacting ethical standards, the force of which carries to this day. Fox's major contribution was not his theology, nor even his encouragement to care for the suffering, important as these were. Rather, it seems to me, what gave durability to the Quaker tradition was the practical result that so many of those who called themselves Friends *behaved more lovingly toward all creatures and assumed an impressive level of responsibility for their society and its institutions.* Perhaps the most innovative result was that, by the effort of those whom Fox inspired, the quality of some contemporary institutions, notably commerce, was markedly improved.[109]

George Fox exemplified a mentoring leader imparting a concern for the environment, animals, people, and to his followers.

In "Dreams Gone Wild: A New Kind of Human," Len Sweet describes a type of leader not focused on self and how success can be achieved, "When you peel away the layers from every "Dream Gone Wild" in the West, the dream is wild about one thing: ME. This one common denominator in every dreamscape is this: MINE is the KINGDOM, MINE is the POWER, MINE is the GLORY. It's only a ME DREAM."[110]

Jesus did not assert his rights as God leading from the position of divine authority; instead He led from the position of a human servant. Those who were mentored by Jesus realized their potential as leaders by observing the power of selflessness and compassion in a world that mentored leaders through military prowess

> Church leaders experienced death threats.

empowered by fear and death and political/religious power established through the centuries.[111] Jesus equipped His followers with the Holy Spirit and mentored them to become servants to those who followed them

Servant Leadership off the Rails

Christianity grew during the first and second centuries despite persecution. During this time, the servant leadership model Jesus had established began to dissolve into a hierarchal model to be sought after by those who wanted control. Church leaders became the 'served' not the ones who served. These leadership positions were sought after because of the personal power and prestige that they offered. From Jesus time until our present day, church leadership continues to establish its identity seemingly always to miss the servant leadership model Jesus presented.

According to Justo Gonzalez, second century church governance "was made up of three distinct positions of leadership: bishop, presbyter—or elder—and deacon."[112] These positions became established church offices and promoted many styles of church government.

Gonzales points out that women filled prominent church leadership roles.

Martin Luther tried to put the sheep under the care of clergy.

Church leadership was male dominated as the second century closed, but this was not true during the first century and a significant part of the second. Gonzalez recalls the story of the Roman governor, Pliny, who told Trajan that he had ordered the torture of two Christian female ministers. Gonzalez suggests that in, "its efforts to combat heresy, the church centralized its authority, and a by-product of that process was that women were excluded from positions of leadership."[113] Male leadership dominated and developed a hierarchal structure of church of power that proved dictatorial and fatal for those who resisted.

Constantine converted to Christianity and issued an edict of toleration toward Christianity, which ultimately became the state religion of the Roman Empire. As it did church leadership grew exponentially. Leadership in the church became self-serving and exploited those whom God had called to care for his sheep. The Reformation jolted the established church and Martin Luther tried to put the sheep under the care of clergy, but he did not return to Jesus' leadership model.

The Enlightenment introduced a new direction of thought, and leaders sought truth through reason, philosophy, and psychology. Enticements to wealth and power increased the distance between the sheep and clergy. Politics and religion ruled with few exceptions. An example of an exception occurred when God worked through the 1801 Cane Ridge Revival[114] and called leaders to preach the gospel and shepherd the people. A Kentucky Presbyterian minister organized the Cane Ridge Revival, and it was a powerful manifestation of God's power. Thousands of Baptists and Methodists gathered, as did some who came to drink, gamble, and carouse. The result was an incredible visitation of God from which camp meetings were born, and many went out to preach the gospel armed only with the knowledge of God's call on their lives and lacking Bible school training.

The Cane Ridge Revival sparked a new evangelism method that produced a pastoral care movement for the converted and emphasized the office of pastor. Pastors visited, taught, and served those in their care as servant leaders based on King David's shepherding metaphor. The new evangelism method resembled the Christ's pattern of leading his disciples.

CEO or Servant Leader?

The church does not need more leaders who seek CEO positions. The church needs servant leaders who lead like Jesus, follow his example, and wash their teammates' feet. Such leaders equip others by walking alongside the team members they mentor. These servant leaders emulate Jesus Christ. The result is leadership in the twenty-first century church without CEOs.

The business model of leadership is powerful and brought changes to the church's focus and operation. The church can be understood as a business, but the business model does not reflect Jesus' original purpose for the church. Ecclesial success is often measured by numerical church growth, new building programs, and increased budgets, but a corporate model creates additional expectations. For example, the senior pastor becomes a CEO, a board of directors replaces the board of deacons/elders, church property is called a campus, and people measure success based on finances.

In *Off-Road Disciplines,* Earl Creps describes Larry who is the chief administrator of a denominational region and very stressed, "Larry wept openly. The pressure of holding together the churches of his region spilled out into our class-room, along with his deep concern that even the best efforts of the regional leadership lacked whatever it takes to bring unity."[115] Larry was overwhelmed by demands that required his knowledge, wisdom, and experience but these demands depleted his compassion reserves. The result was CF.

Many current leadership books promote business modeled for twenty-first century churches. Experts hold seminars, coaches develop church leaders, professional fundraisers help meet the financial goals, and churches hire successful leaders who model their ministries after other successful leaders. They build mega churches and establish staff for pastors of media, worship, visual arts, hospitality, family counseling, young adults, young married, singles, and so on. They spend millions of dollars annually to develop a twenty-first century church organization and its leadership, but overall church attendance continues dropping.

Len Sweet states in *The Church of the Perfect Storm:*

In Europe, Christians are almost an endangered species. At the same time that Christianity is dying in the West, Christianity is surging in the East and in the South. The statistical center of Christianity today is in Timbuktu, Mali. The language of Christianity today is Spanish; the color of Christianity today is not white, but brown; and there are more churches in India today than in the United States.[116]

The church is in North America is dying in spite of statistical insight, wealth, expert training, professional advertising, seminary/business school educated leadership, state-of-the-art buildings, the latest technology, and the best musicians and songwriters. As a result of the pressure, church leaders may develop a messiah complex feeling they are responsible for the success of the church and causing them to work harder while sacrificing self care and family time resulting in CF. The original plan for church leadership was the calling and equipping of church leaders through the Holy Spirit of God. The apostle Paul describes this calling:

And He gave some as apostles, and some as prophets, and some as evangelists, and some as pastors and teachers, for the equipping of the saints for the work of service, to the building up of the body of Christ; until we all attain to the unity of the faith, and of the knowledge of the Son of God, to a mature man, to the measure of the stature which belongs to the fullness of Christ. (Ephesians 4:11-13)

The Holy Spirit provides the power to accomplish this as we see in the next chapter.

Shabbat
Relax and Re-Create

Are you doing what God has summoned you to do?

How much of your stress is caused your leadership style?

Take the Birkman personality assessment and have your leadership take it as well. What does it show you about how you lead? What does your team look like in comparison to you?
http://www.birkman.com/birkmanMethod/whatIs-TheBirkmanMethod.php

Read The Starfish and the Spider. Is your leadership style hierarchal or team based? Do you need the recognition of your title?

Take a piece of paper and entitle it, "WHO I AM." Describe who you are in bullet point form. Remember: you are who you are, not what you do.

CHAPTER FIVE

DOING CHURCH WITHOUT GOD: THE NEED FOR THE HOLY SPIRIT'S WORK IN CHURCH LEADERS' LIVES

Now Jesus, full of the Holy Spirit, left the Jordan and was led by the Spirit into the wild. For forty wilderness days and nights He was tested by the Devil... That completed the testing. The Devil retreated temporarily, lying in wait for another opportunity. Jesus returned to Galilee powerful in the Spirit.

Luke 4:1-2, 13-15 (Message)

Jesus entered His ministry "full of the Holy Spirit" having endured forty days of spiritual war-

> "How many of you can do church without God?"

fare with Satan (Luke 4:1-13). He returned to Galilee after his forty-day fast "in the power of the Holy Spirit" (Luke 4:14) that produced power, gifts, and fruit. Many church leaders today operate from their own abilities and gifts and charismatic personalities. Driven by the machinery of ministry they neglect to draw from the Holy Spirit's power and soon find themselves in a deficit position as a result of self imposed agendas and a desire to accomplish great things for God without relying totally upon him for their strength. I believe it is imperative that leaders learn to function in the power of the Holy Spirit (Acts 1:8) His gifts (Romans 12:6-8, 1 Corinthians 12:4-11, Ephesians 4:7-14) and the end result will be the fruit He produces in the lives of His followers (Galatians 5:22-23). By doing so, it will significantly reduce the possibility of CF.

In a workshop entitled *Theology and Practice of the Baptism of the Holy Spirit* presented at the BC/Yukon PAOC District Conference on the Ministry a group of seasoned church leaders we were asked, "How many of you can do church without God?"[117] Some hesitated, but eventually all raised their hand. Church leaders may enter ministry on their own power but leave ministry emptied of all power. God called and empowered countless leaders from Adam to Moses, David, and Jesus, the disciples, the Cane Ridge Revival participants, the Azusa Street revivalists, and members of the Twentieth Century charismatic movement. God's intention is that church leaders reflect the servant-ministry of Jesus by way of the power of the Holy Spirit. I believe the contemporary church is desperate for a new leadership paradigm empowered by the Holy Spirit. In many cases, the Holy Spirit is the missing component in contemporary church leadership. Ministry based on personal power and experience but lacking the power of the Holy Spirit will produce CF.

> The caution is becoming His hands, but operating from our own power.

A Form of Godliness?

In *So Beautiful*, Leonard Sweet wrote about ministry in the contemporary church using the medical metaphor of the MRI or Magnetic Resonance Imaging procedure which is used in many hospitals to examine the human body. Sweet's MRI is a formula that can be used by leaders to examine the health of the body of Christ. Sweet's 'M' stands for missional referring to the *mind* of God. God's plan for church leadership is to 'equip the saints for the work of ministry' (Ephesians 4:12a) and to bring the good news to the lost. I believe it is possible to quip the body of Christ to do the work of ministry without the Holy Spirit. Programs, seminars, graduate and post graduate degrees combined with years of personal ministry provide the academic and experiential component of training. When church leaders attempt to equip the saints without drawing completely upon the power of the Holy Spirit CF can result.

Sweet's 'R' is in reference to the *heart* of God. Relationship is God's ultimate goal. In relationship we connect with one another, and connecting opens the door to intimacy. God desires relationship with His creation. In the extreme sense of the word, God sent His Son in human form to connect with His children in an intimate and personal way. This relationship allows God and His creation to develop trust and intimacy with one another. Sadly, church leaders that are called to equip parishioners can replicate this 'relational' connection with one another without the empowerment of the Holy Spirit. Similar to the missional aspect of the MRI, church leaders are able to develop and nurture the relational aspect of equipping the body by their own charisma, personality, previous training or experience and to do so without the Holy Spirit. As a result, the church leader becomes susceptible to CF by not drawing upon the power of the Holy Spirit.

Sweet's 'I' stands for Incarnational which refers to the *hands* of God. "Incarnation is what God's hands are up to."[118] Incarnational ministry is ministry empowered by the Holy Spirit. This is the one section of the MRI that is impossible to do without the empowerment of the Holy Spirit. Incarnational ministry is central to leadership. Leaders who minister from their own ability (power) will discover it is wholly inadequate for the task. This inevitably leads to Compassion Fatigue. God alone empowers Christian ministry, and when he does, the church will function as the mind, heart and hands of God. Church leadership needs an MRI scan to reveal their spiritual health.

I believe the church is suffering today because leaders are neglecting the power of the Holy Spirit and relying more upon methods, models and perspiration. Before his ascension, Jesus spoke to his followers about the promise of the Holy Spirit. He contended that same Spirit would empower them for their ministries:

> Gathering them together, He commanded them not to leave Jerusalem, but to wait for what the Father had promised, "Which," He said, "you heard of from Me; for John baptized with water, but you will be baptized with the Holy Spirit not many days from now . . . but you will receive power when the Holy Spirit has come upon you; and you shall be My witnesses

both in Jerusalem, and in all Judea and Samaria, and even to the remotest part of the earth. (Acts 1:4-5, 8)

The following is a personal MRI review of two church leadership conferences that I attended back to back in the spring of 2008. Attending these reminded me of the need for the Holy Spirit's power and anointing on the church and its leadership. During the first conference, the speakers encouraged attendees to express themselves artistically during the plenary sessions. They were exhorted to focus their worship on dance, poetry, and multimedia presentations.

> Only God's power through the gospel changes lives eternally.

I was somewhat uncomfortable, due in great part to my religious cultural background which considers artistic expressions distractive. The conference speakers' emphasis on this style of liturgy was foreign to me. My worship tradition arose from a very different liturgical heritage.

> Looking backward may be ineffective in moving the church forward.

I detected a measure of moderate spiritual anarchy from the speakers during the conference. For example, plenary speakers and workshop presenters suggested that twenty-first century church survival depended on movement away from a hierarchal form of ecclesial government and its emphasis on buildings and denominational structures. The speakers suggested a return to a monastic form of worship, house churches, a missional focus, with a social gospel emphasis.

I appreciate the need for change in the church and recognize that our methods are becoming ineffective for the cause of Christ, especially in North America. I worry, however, that liturgy with visual, auditory, and olfactory stimuli are not in and of themselves able satisfy our spiritual hunger. I worry that they may not stimulate people's desire for a personal relationship with Christ. The idea of house meetings rather than church buildings and leaderless organizations are not new. It all begs the question, 'change is inevitable, but what change will be effective? I believe the conference took a "retro" view of the church. However, looking backward may not move the church effectively forward. I was disappointed as I felt the conference presented nothing new or innovative. It did not explain how we can impact the world with Christ's message. The conference's critical missing piece was the Holy Spirit's work and power. Instead, the conference focused on what *people* can do. It was wonderful and appeared godly, but lacked power.

Two days later I attended our denomination's annual conference. This four day gathering emphasized the Holy Spirit's influence in ministry. The theme of the conference was, "Authentic and Passionate Pentecostal Spirituality." The conference focused on the Holy Spirit's contemporary work and emphasized pneumatological aspects and their practical applications.

I felt spiritually energized by the plenary sessions and workshops. Unlike the previous conference, speakers emphasized what the Holy Spirit could do through us as willing and obedient leaders. They recounted what happened as the Holy Spirit moved through the decades from the birth of our movement at the Azuza Street Revival in the early 1900's to the present. Then they focused on what the Holy Spirit is doing now.

Conference speakers described how the Spirit driven church can impact our world. I was impressed with their sensitivity to our world's needs. They conveyed how the church should address politics and the needs of the poor and environmental conditions. However, they emphasized that it is only through the power of the Holy Spirit that the gospel message can change lives eternally. Individuals who desire an encounter with the God of creation are invited to become part of the family of God through the Spirit of Adoption (Romans 8:15) with the Holy Spirit bearing witness that we are children of God. (Romans 8:16).

I believe the New Testament church Jesus created for His disciples was an extreme church that depended upon the power of the Holy Spirit. For example, Jesus told his disciples to go to Jerusalem and wait for the Father to empower them. Because of their obedience to his instructions, the power of the Holy Spirit was evident in these leaders and the church they served

I believe the Holy Spirit's presence and power are as in today's church as they were in the New Testament church. I don't believe God has changed his strategy for the church. The Holy Spirit must operate in the leadership of the contemporary church in order to impact individual believers and the corporate body.

His Work in the Individual Believer

The church is not a building or an organization, but a living organism with a definite composition. The Apostle Paul frequently referred to the church as a body and individuals make up the body, "For just as the body is one and have many members, and all the members of the body, though many are one body, so it is with Christ. For in the one Spirit we were all baptized into one body—Jews or Greeks, slaves or free—and we were all made to drink of one Spirit" (1 Corinthians 12:12-13). The Holy Spirit plays an essential part in the lives of individual members of his body, as we will see in the next few pages.

Indwelling

The wonderful work of the Holy Spirit does not end with regeneration (salvation) because the Spirit dwells in believers during their earthly lives. Because he dwells within us, we begin a process of sanctification. "And the very God of peace **sanctify** you wholly; and I pray God your whole spirit and soul and body be preserved blameless unto the coming of our Lord Jesus Christ" (1 Thessalonians 5:23 KJV). The Holy Spirit works in the life of believers to bring them to a proper reflection of Jesus Christ.

The book of John refers to the Spirit as the "paraclete," the One who comes along side, "And I will ask the Father, and He will give you another advocate to help you and be with you forever—the Spirit of truth. The world cannot accept Him, because it neither sees Him nor knows Him. But you know Him, for He lives with you and will be in you." (John 14:16, 17). L. Thomas Holdcroft in his book, *The Holy Spirit,* suggests that the modern synonyms for Paraclete include, "instructor, guide, advocate, ombudsman, partaker, interpreter, advice knows Him; but you know Him, for He dwells with giver, governor, assistant, helper, attorney, and barrister."[119] The Apostle Paul writes to the Corinthian church and reminds them that they are "the temple of the Holy Spirit" (1 Corinthians 3:16). Church leaders must avail themselves of the many aspects of the Holy Spirit, relying on him completely to fulfill their ministry through His power.

Millard Erickson describes his understanding of the Spirit's indwelling work in all believers, "The Spirit, however, is able to affect one more intensely because, dwelling within; He can get to the very center of one's thinking and emotions. By indwelling believers, the Spirit can lead them into all truth, as Jesus promised."[120] The Holy Spirit is not to be warehoused within the believer, simply placed on a shelf and never accessed. Instead he must become the reservoir of power from which all expressions of the church leader's ministry finds its power. Jesus described the Holy Spirit as a river of living water (John 7:38) that flows from a person's innermost being, "But this he [Jesus] spoke concerning the Spirit, whom those believing in Him would receive; for the Holy Spirit was not yet given, because Jesus was not yet glorified (John 7:39).

In *Untranslatable Riches from the Greek New Testament,* Kenneth S. Wuest writes about the Holy Spirit's empowerment of believers, "It is not that . . . believer[s use] the power of God but that God's power uses [them]. . . . The power of the Holy Spirit is potentially resident in the saint by virtue of His indwelling presence, but it is operative in . . . believer[s] when [they yield] to and depend upon the ministry of the Spirit."[121] It is not that believers have more of the Holy Spirit when they receive Holy Spirit's baptism, but that the Spirit has more of them. The more intimate believers become with the Holy Spirit, the more they trust him. The more they trust him, the more willingly they obey Him. The more willingly they obey him, the more often they find themselves in the favor of God. The more often they find themselves in the favor of God, the less stress they experience in their lives and ministry. This empowerment process reduces the risk of CF.

Jesus commissions his followers to this Spirit empowered ministry in the gospel of John when he says, "Truly,

truly, I say to you, he who believes in Me, the works that I do, he will do also; and greater works than these he will do; because I go to the Father." (John 14:12). Following his discourse on love and commitment, grafting and pruning (John 15), Jesus reminds his followers, during the Feast of Tabernacles, of his promised Holy Spirit would be given in Jerusalem enabling each of them to fulfill this commission through the power of the Holy Spirit in their lives (John 7:37-39).

Pentecost: the Church on Fire

After his resurrection, Jesus told his followers to wait in Jerusalem, of the five hundred that he told (1 Corinthians 15:6, Acts 1:3-5) one hundred and twenty gathered in the upper room (Acts 1:15). The apostles and those gathered with them were waiting for the Holy Spirit in expectation, not understanding the dynamic change that was to take place in their lives and their ministries. Their willingness and obedience to wait was one of dependence upon the power of God. The apostles knowing their inability to minister without God's power in their lives and so in faith they drew near to God in expectation.

As leaders we must be conscious of our need for the power of the Holy Spirit in our lives personally and for ministry. Jesus described the process by which the gift of the Father would come; it was a new kind of baptism. John had baptized the repentant in water, an external declaration of an inward change, now Jesus would baptize these same believers internally with the power of the Holy Spirit (Acts 1:4, 5). Following the Holy Spirit baptism, the apostles and those who gathered with them entered into ministry enabled by the power and the anointing of the Holy Spirit.

Baptism for repentance called for the believer to be *immersed* into the water where as baptism of the Holy Spirit called for the believer to be filled with the water of the Spirit that would then come forth from them. Water baptism was a complete covering of the outside of the body and the new Holy Spirit baptism would be a complete inner-self baptism. Jesus words, "out of your innermost being will flow rivers of living water" described the freedom of the Holy Spirit resident within the believer released to empower Spirit anointed ministry to take place in the believer's life (John 7:37-39). When this is activated in the church leader's life, they become a vessel of the Holy Spirit through which ministry can pour out.

When Jesus had finished with this directive to his followers he was lifted up and a cloud received him. The promise was given that he would return the same way he left. A few short days later, Jesus baptized everyone in the upper room and they were empowered for ministry (Matthew 3:11c).

The church was born with fire. John the Baptist prophesied that Jesus would baptize the church with the Holy Spirit and fire (Matthew 3:11). The precious gift of the Holy Spirit was given on the Day of Pentecost and he came with both audio and visual signs. The sound of a mighty wind was heard by the obedient that waited for the gift of the Father. Luke records that the entire house where they were sitting was filled the sound of the Holy Spirit. (Acts 2:2b). He also records the manifestations of the tongues like fire coming to rest on the apostles and others who had gathered with them.

Fire and wind are symbolic of the presence and power the Holy Spirit. Throughout Scripture the presence of God is represented in symbols such as fire, wind and a cloud. Moses experienced a burning bush, (Exodus 3:2) a cloud and a pillar of fire (Exodus 13:21) as well as a powerful wind that blew an escape route through the Red Sea, bringing deliverance for the Hebrew people (Exodus 14:21). The culmination of these symbols on the day of Pentecost accentuates the presence of Holy Spirit in the upper room that day. The prophet Joel prophesied about an outpouring of the Holy Spirit on all mankind (Joel 2:28, 29). This manifestation of the supernatural, the sound of a mighty wind, the sight of the tongues of fire on the obedient and then the obedient speaking in languages they did not know was a demonstration of God's divine power over the natural power of mankind.

There was a visual manifestation of fire resting upon the heads of everyone in the upper room. This fire did not remain as a visual expression of the power of God, but manifested itself in a new way through strength and boldness allowing the gospel message to pour forth from men and women in a miraculous form; speaking in unknown languages. The manifestation of the wind and the fire became like a wildfire that burned its way into the hearts of those who heard. The result of this miracle was an encounter with God. People who knew God had been empowered by the Holy Spirit to cross natural barriers and share the message of salvation with people who did not know God. This was a divine reversal of the confusion of languages at the Tower of Babel (Genesis 11:6, 7). Instead of language dividing and separating mankind from God, a supernatural ability to communicate in all languages now spoke eternal life into his creation. The church was born in a spiritual inferno that would generate power for the church until the return of Christ.

As a result, the obedient were empowered to preach the good news and the unconverted were mesmerized as they heard the message of salvation in their own language. The purpose of the Holy Spirit baptism is *missional*; the presence of the Holy Spirit resident in the believer is *Incarnational*. Those filled with the Holy Spirit began taking the gospel to the entire world (Matthew 28:19) as they ministered in the power of the Holy Spirit (Acts 1:8) making disciples of all nations. This baptism in the Holy Spirit empowered the called to a level of anointing in their lives that they had previously never experienced. Peter the disciple became Peter the leader as a result of the baptism of the Holy Spirit.

Spirit Empowered Leadership

Luke records that following Peter's sermon on the Day of Pentecost to the same crowd over three thousand people made a decision to follow Christ (Acts 2:41) and the church began to grow because of the power of the Holy Spirit. His life was completely changed. Before being baptized in the Holy Spirit Peter vehemently denied his connection to Christ

(John 18:25-27) but after he was baptized in the Holy Spirit he preached a powerful sermon to the enemies of Christ even calling them to account for the death of their Messiah (Acts 2: 13-41). Peter's ministry was Holy Spirit empowered and the anointing is evident in the lives of the people throughout the book of Acts. Facing ridicule, rejection and/or the possibility of death, Peter spoke to the crowd in Jerusalem. All of whom had just witnessed the Holy Spirit's supernatural manifestation of power through these freshly Holy Spirit baptized evangelists.

This new anointing on Peter's life was twofold. First, it gave him a new boldness to preach the gospel allowing it to accomplish its life changing message (Acts 2:37) and second it was the source of miracles to deliver such a message and lead the church of Christ in power, neither of which could be self-generated. In Acts Chapter Three, when Peter and John were on their way to the Temple for prayer they encountered a man desiring healing. Peter took him by the hand, lifted him up and said, "Silver and gold I do not have, but what I have I give you..." (Acts 3: 6, 7). The prophet Zechariah spoke to Zerubbabel instructing him that effective ministry emanates solely from God not man's abilities, experience, charisma or personal strength, it is, "not by might, not by power, but by my Spirit, says the Lord." (Zechariah 4: 6). Living from this perspective may bring longevity, health and divine rhythm to a leader's life, reducing the risk of CF.

The Apostle Paul's letter to the Romans (Romans 8:9-11) [122]reminds the reader to die to the natural life and live in the Spirit empowered life. The church leader cannot rely on natural gifting, experience, education or programs to be effective in ministry. Instead, Paul encourages them to depend completely on the Holy Spirit to bring life to their ministry, allowing Spirit-empowered ministry to flow through them. Paul in humility offers to his readers the core strength of his ministry, not eloquent speech, not wisdom, strength or persuasive language, but, "a demonstration of the Spirit's power." (1 Corinthians 2:1-5). When the church leader partners with the Holy Spirit there is a significant reduction in stress for the leader and an exceptional healthy environment created for the church leaders and his/her followers.

Paul was well qualified to lead. If anyone could place their confidence in human credentials and experience it would be Paul. In his epistle to the Philippians he lists his credentials identifying himself as a Hebrew from the tribe of Benjamin; an Israelite circumcised on the eighth day (suggesting he was blameless as to adherence to the law). As for zeal, Paul writes that he persecuted the church before his conversion (3:5-7). Yet Paul addressed the Corinthian church in his first letter saying, "My conversation and my preaching were not with persuasive words of wisdom, but with a demonstration of the Spirit and of power, so that your faith would not be based on human wisdom but on the power of God." (I Corinthians 2:1-5).

Paul boldly modeled his reliance on the Holy Spirit and encouraged all leaders to do the same (1 Corinthians 11:1). In his discourse to his followers concerning living a righteous and holy life, he inferred that this righteous and holy life must be one empowered by the Spirit, just as Christ's life was empowered by the Holy Spirit. (Romans 8:11) Paul's conversion was an encounter with Jesus followed by an infilling of the Holy Spirit (Acts 9:3-19a). His life was a living example of obedience, giftedness and Spiritual fruit.

Church leaders must lead with, 'a demonstration of the Spirit and of power' allowing the supernatural to guide and direct the fulfillment of their ministries. This Spirit empowerment in the leader supersedes all natural ability and experience reducing the need to lead by human effort alone. The reduction of human effort results in the reduction of stress resulting in a reduction for the risk of CF.

The Holy Spirit is the source of power for the church leader. He does so by providing charismata or gifts equipping the leader with the 'demonstration of power' as mentioned above and also develops the leader's character to reflect Christ through the fruit of the Holy Spirit. The gifts are distributed as the Holy Spirit determines (1 Corinthians 12:11, I Peter 4:10) but the fruit is resident in the believer upon the initial presence of the Holy Spirit in their lives. The gifts are a vehicle to present the power of God to a lost world and the fruit of the Spirit shapes the leader to reflect the Giver of Gifts, Jesus.

The Fruit of the Spirit

The character of the believer is enhanced by the fruit of the Holy Spirit. Character could be likened to a tree from which the fruit hangs. The Holy Spirit transforms the believer's character and the result is Spiritual fruit. God provides the gifts for doing. God provides the fruit for being. Peter Wagner wrote in *Your Spiritual Gifts Can Help Your Church Grow,* "Fruit is not discovered like the gifts, it is developed through the believer's walk with God and through yieldedness to the Holy Spirit. While spiritual gifts help define what a Christian *does*, the fruit of the Spirit helps define what a Christian *is*."[123]

The fruit of the Holy Spirit becomes more evident as believers mature in Christ. As

> The fruit of the Holy Spirit is not optional.

Christians mature, they reveal their Christ-like characters to those in their sphere of influence. Leaders who mature in the Holy Spirit reflect Christ's character and focus less on "doing ministry in their own strength." This reduces personal striving.

Paul describes the fruit of the Holy Spirit in his letter to the Galatians after his teaching on sinful human nature. Paul contrasts humanity's sinful nature and its corrupt character with the fruit produced by regeneration through the Holy Spirit, "But the fruit of the Spirit is love, joy, peace, patience, kindness, goodness, faithfulness, gentleness, and self-control. Against such things there is no law. Those who belong to Christ Jesus have crucified the sinful nature with its passions and desires. Since we live by the Spirit, let us keep in step with the Spirit." (Galatians 5:22-25). The fruit of the Holy Spirit is the product of sanctification through the Spirit's intervention. Unlike the gifts, the fruit of the Spirit is not optional. It is a reflection of the character of the Holy

Spirit resident in the believer's life. When I realized that the fruit of the Spirit is a believer's life was love and has eight components, I immediately went and peeled an orange, hoping that all oranges would have only eight sections. This would allow me to use a wonderful theological metaphor for the fruit of the spirit. I was greatly disappointed that each orange I dissected had differing numbers of sections, and the metaphor proved unsustainable. But, in contrast to the differing number of sections of the orange, the Holy Spirit is consistent in producing all fruit within the believer as he/she matures.

The concept that the fruit of the Spirit is love and this love is a composite of characteristics of God gives the believer confidence that as they mature they will become more like God; for God is Love. Paul in Chapter Thirteen of First Corinthians describes the fruit of the Spirit being love:

> If I speak in the tongues of men or of angels, but do not have love, I am only a resounding gong or a clanging cymbal. If I have the gift of prophecy and can fathom all mysteries and all knowledge, and if I have a faith that can move mountains, but do not have love, I am nothing. If I give all I possess to the poor and give over my body to hardship that I may boast, but do not have love, I gain nothing. Love is patient, love is kind. It does not envy, it does not boast, it is not proud. It does not dishonor others, it

is not self-seeking, it is not easily angered, it keeps no record of wrongs. Love does not delight in evil but rejoices with the truth. It always protects, always trusts, always hopes, always perseveres. Love never fails. But where there are prophecies, they will cease; where there are tongues, they will be stilled; where there is knowledge, it will pass away. For we know in part and we prophesy in part, but when completeness comes, what is in part disappears. When I was a child, I talked like a child, I thought like a child, I reasoned like a child. When I became a man, I put the ways of childhood behind me. For now we see only a reflection as in a mirror; then we shall see face to face. Now I know in part; then I shall know fully, even as I am fully known. And now these three remain: faith, hope and love. But the greatest of these is love. (1 Corinthians 13)

This passage reveals much about Christian character and describes our source of strength as rooted and grounded in God. Allowing the Holy Spirit to reflect Christ in our lives and ministry overcomes fear and weakness that depletes confidence, emotions, and faith. The lives of church leaders must reflect the inner working of the Holy Spirit; neglect of the Holy Spirit's fruit will stimulate dependency on personal strength and character leading to stress and the risk of CF.

The Gifts of the Spirit

The Holy Spirit dwells in regenerate believers and bestows gifts upon them. Peter confirmed that all followers of Christ receive at least one or more special gifts from God and these gifts are to be used to serve others, "Each one should use whatever gift he has received to serve others, faithfully administering God's grace in its various forms..." (1 Peter 4:10). In his letter to the Ephesians, Paul identifies five specific gifts. Apostles, prophets, evangelists, pastors and teachers are for equipping of the church to carry out the ministry (Ephesians 4: 8-13). These are recognized today in the church as leadership positions.

The importance of Paul's statement in Ephesians does not lie in the type of gift as much as the purpose of the gift. The gifts of equipping indicate that they are given to specific individuals to develop and equip the members of Christ's body to do the work of ministry. Neglecting the purpose of the gift or relying on one's own experience and natural skills will cause the church leader to become overwhelmed with the magnitude of ministry and attempt to' run the race' (Hebrews 12:1) in their own strength. This makes them susceptible to the debilitating effects of CF.

In *Tragedy in the Church: The Missing Gifts*, A. W. Tozer
contends that the human body is the perfect metaphor for
the church. Tozer discusses Paul's teaching about the Holy
Spirit's gifts within the body of Christ and how members
receive and use their gifts for God's glory:

> A careful study of the Apostle's teaching concerning
> Jesus Christ and his church should persuade us that
> any local assembly ought to demonstrate all of the
> functions of the whole body. Paul clearly teaches that
> each believer ought to demonstrate a proper gift or
> gifts, bestowed by God and the Holy Spirit, and that
> together the believers would accomplish the work of
> God as a team.[124]

Tozer emphasizes the diversity and importance of the Spirits'
gifts among members of Christ's body expressing that
the members must function together as a team. This team
must include the Holy Spirit as its Director Team ministry
reduces ministry stress and lessens the risk of CF especially
if the source of strength for the leader is the Holy Spirit. The
Holy Spirit's gifts work in and through Christians to bless
and encourage God's people and non-Christians alike.

The Holy Spirit's gifts vary among believers. Paul in
his epistle to the Romans his first letter to the Corinthians
includes lists of gifts. In Romans (12:4, 5) he prefaces his list

with a description of the body of Christ and how numerous members with different functions belong to one another and operate through God's grace by the Spirit of God. The list is diverse: prophesying, serving, teaching, encouraging, giving, leadership, and showing mercy. In First Corinthians Paul introduces his list as reminder that the gifts are given, "as a manifestation of the Spirit for the benefit of all." (12:7). Paul wrote, "There are different kinds of gifts, but the same Spirit. There are different kinds of service, but the same Lord. There are different kinds of working, but the same God works all of them in all men" (1 Corinthians 12:4-6); indicating that the gifts are empowered by the Holy Spirit. Paul lists nine gifts in First Corinthians: the word of wisdom, the word of knowledge, the gift of faith, divine healing, the working of miracles, the word of prophecy, the distinguishing of spirits, speaking in different kinds of tongues, and the interpretation of tongues. These gifts are used to equip believers for service in ministry. As leaders, being equipped with the correct tools does not guarantee that one will not suffer from burnout or compassion fatigue. There is a need for grace and personal contentment.

A skilled leader is able to use his/her gifts successfully in ministry and yet not feel that they have accomplished any tangible evidence of this success. Unlike a carpenter who builds a house and upon completion stands back and sees the completed project, church leaders seldom see tangible evidence of their ministry effort. This can be discouraging and may lead to discouragement, depression, and burnout or compassion fatigue.

For the leader in crisis, it is not an issue of working longer or using their gifts more often, but it is finding contentment in the knowledge that they are functioning in their calling in obedience to God and he is pleased with their ministry efforts. A tangible suggestion for the church leader or care giver to bring a sense of completion in their life is to work with inanimate objects during your off time. Some of these may include other gifts and talents that they may have such as: painting, music, woodworking, sculpture, writing, gardening and so on. Such nurturing of one's self develops a healthy spirituality and provides a strong framework for the fruit of the Holy Spirit which will be evident in the leader's life.

Holy Spirit Anointing

Empowerment in the operation of these gifts comes though the unction or anointing of the Holy Spirit (I John

2:27). The Holy Spirit flows through willing and obedient believers spiritually empowering them to operate in the supernatural. Anointing in the Old Testament occurred utilizing such substances as oil, myrrh, and/or balsam. Anointing symbolized the recognition of position and power in the Old Testament. People were anointed for office through a procedure of pouring oil on the candidate, and many contemporary churches continue this practice. David, the shepherd boy anointed as the king of Israel, drew an analogy between God's followers as the flocks of sheep tended and cared for by shepherds, "You anoint my head with oil; my cup overflows" (Psalm 23:5b). Oil was poured on sheep to refresh them, protect them from disease, and seal all open wounds. The anointing David referred to was that of healing, care and protection provided by a loving Shepherd. However, anointing also conveys authority and position.

Ronald F. Youngblood explains the connection between Old and New Testament anointing, "This (New Testament) anointing is not only for kings, priests, and prophets; it is for everyone who believes in the Lord Jesus Christ. But this is also a spiritual anointing, as the Holy Spirit anoints a person's heart and mind with the love and truth of God."[125] Holdcroft believes, "the anointed believer is more competent to communicate God's message, not merely because his mind is stimulated, but because there is a divine accuracy, authority, honesty and efficiency to his words."[126] Holdcroft and Youngblood remind leaders that effective ministry results from willingness and obedience to the Holy Spirit allowing Him to empower them to use their gifts for the equipping of the body of Christ. According to Holdcroft, "This anointing is not a special favor, but the ordinary outcome of his presence and indwelling. Because the believer is anointed, he may undertake the Great Commission, and whatever personal calls to service may be his as well."[127] Jesus was anointed in the Holy Spirit when He used words of knowledge and wisdom speaking truth into the life of woman at the well (John 4:10-26). The result of this encounter with Jesus changed her life significantly and she retuned back to her home town and told everyone about the Messiah (John 4:28-30).

Jesus changed the lives of His disciples on a daily basis. As these followers found themselves in the presence of the Master, they were called to minister to the both Jew and Gentile. Jesus called them to follow Him and then sent them out with all power and authority Luke describes how He sent the 'twelve' out to preach, "...giving them power and authority over all demons and to heal diseases. And He sent them out to proclaim the kingdom of God, and to perform healing." (Luke 9:1, 2). Luke continues to describe the seventy who were sent out two by two for ministry, "having given them authority...over all power of the enemy and nothing shall injure you." (Luke 10: 19).

The book of Acts presents us with the lives of many key leaders who under the anointing of the Holy Spirit accomplished mighty things for God. Three of these stand out to the author. First, Peter, the head of the New Testament Church was transformed by the baptism of the Holy Spirit (Acts 2:1-41) into a powerful early church leader. Second, Phillip, the evangelist reached the multitudes because of "the signs and great miracles taking place." (Acts 8; 5-17). Third, Paul powerfully converted by an encounter with Jesus (Acts 9:1-9) and the baptized in the Holy Spirit (Acts 9:17-18) was used by God to bring the message of salvation to the Gentiles.

The Apostle Peter

Peter is our first example of one of Jesus' followers ministering in the anointing of the Holy Spirit. Luke records that he stood up, raised his voice and addressed the mocking crowd convicting them of their sin and calling them to repentance (Acts 2:40, 41). Shortly after Peter and John are anointed they are used by God to heal a lame man at the Gate Beautiful (Acts 3:1-10). They soon had to defend themselves against the priests, the commander of the temple and Sadducees. When questioned, Peter, full of the Holy Spirit, spoke under the anointing in their defense (Acts 4:8-12). When Peter was confronted with the sin of Ananias and Sapphira, he discerned they had lied to the Holy Spirit (Acts 5:5-10). Following God's judgment on Ananias and Sapphira, Luke noted that the apostles were anointed to cast out demons and heal the sick. Even Peter's shadow became a vessel of the Holy Spirit's anointing, healing all who came into contact with it (Acts 5:15).

Phillip the Evangelist

Phillip, a disciple of Christ, was known for his obedience and boldness. He was called by Jesus and given, "authority over unclean spirits the power to heal." (Matthew 10:1-4). Philip was present in the upper room (Acts 1:13) when the Holy Spirit filled all who were gathered (Acts 2:1-4) experi-

encing the power and anointing of the Holy Spirit in his life
and the lives of his fellow disciples. The Holy Spirit empowered Philip in different gifts
such as: discernment, when

> The Holy Spirit leads
> and guides His people.

dealing with Simon the magi-
cian (Acts 8:17-23), signs and miracles displaying the power
of God in his preaching (Acts 8:13) and giving him boldness
to obey God when He sent him to preach to the Ethiopian
eunuch (Acts 8: 26-40).

The Apostle Paul

The Apostle Paul knew how the Holy Spirit could
change lives. After his encounter with Jesus on the road
to Damascus, his life was changed from a persecutor of
believers (Acts 9:3-6) to one who was called and empowered by the Holy Spirit to equip the church. (9:17-19) Paul
depended totally on the Holy Spirit trusting him completely
with his life, "Now when they had gone through Phrygia and
the region of Galatia, they were forbidden by the Holy Spirit
to preach the word in Asia. After they had come to Mysia,
they tried to go into Bithynia, but the Spirit did not permit
them" (Acts 16:6-7). Paul knew that his life and ministry had

to be completely governed and directed by the Holy Spirit. Paul wrote to the Roman Church:

> You, however, are not in the realm of the flesh but are in the realm of the Spirit, if indeed the Spirit of God lives in you. And if anyone does not have the Spirit of Christ, they do not belong to Christ. But if Christ is in you, then even though your body is subject to death because of sin, the Spirit gives life because of righteousness. And if the Spirit of him who raised Jesus from the dead is living in you, he who raised Christ from the dead will also give life to your mortal bodies because of his Spirit who lives in you. (Romans 8:9-11)

Church leaders are capable of doing church without God. Jesus began his earthly ministry 'full of the Holy Ghost' and continued throughout his ministry in that same power. It is essential that church leaders are empowered by the Holy Spirit in their fulfillment of ministry, neglecting the Holy Spirit, "leads to having a form of godliness but denying its power." (1Timothy 3:5). The Holy Spirit works in the life of the individual by indwelling the believer, becoming an accessible reservoir of power. The believer is equipped with gifts that demonstrate the omnipotence of God and the Fruit of the Holy Spirit through which the church leader reflecting the character of God. His anointing upon the believer releases divine power through an earthen vessel. This anointing is an integral component that provides a conduit of power and strength to the leader. Church leaders who expect to avoid compassion fatigue's debilitating effects must not only observe the Sabbath develop good self-care skill, embrace Christ's servant leadership model, but seek the Holy Spirit's anointing for direction, power, and wisdom for their ministry.

God calls believers into leadership. When leaders trust God and obey his call they find strength and peace in the Holy Spirit in every situation within that calling. This assurance of his call and his anointing on the church leader combined with proper emotional and physical self care offer a balanced lifestyle. Balance in these areas of life, spirit, body and soul; offset the debilitating effects of Compassion Fatigue. The next chapter addresses this balance in the leader's life.

Shabbat
Relax and Re-Create

Meditate on the idea of a "God Encounter" where the Holy Spirit moves outside the normal church program. What would that look like? How would this relieve your personal stress?

As a leader, can you "do church without God?"

Is the Holy Spirit the source of your power for life and ministry? If not, what empowers you?

What is/are your gift/gifts? Read: Romans 12, I Corinthians 12, and Ephesians 4. Write down your gift or gifts. Make a list of other gifts the Lord has worked through you.

Knowing the fruits of the Holy Spirit are not optional in believers' lives, what fruits have you the most difficulty developing to maturity. Why?

What does knowing "the Holy Spirit dwells within you" mean to you?

Psalm 23 is familiar to most church leaders. What areas of this psalm do you allow the Shepherd of your life to care for you? What areas need his care in your life?

CHAPTER SIX

THERE IS A GOD AND
YOU'RE ARE NOT HIM

> What is it about the "ministry" that can compel a
> person to try and do more than Jesus did?
> > Eric T. Scalise, "When Helping You
> > Is Hurting Me"

I had Friday off. I promised my thirteen year old daughter we would go horseback riding with her in the afternoon. The sun warmed the air and the idea of riding through the farmland near our home was inviting. I saddled the horses

> I told the congregation I was always available. Just call'

and came back into the house when the phone rang. I thought if I answered the call it would probably mean that the horseback ride was off. I pastored a small church and people often phoned with needs regardless of the day or time. As a servant leader I expected this because I told the congregation that I was always available: "Just call."

I looked at the ringing phone and then at my daughter's face. She looked disappointed and said loudly, without uttering a word, "If

> She informed me that God had intervened; her situation was under control.

you pick up that phone, we won't be going riding." I picked up the phone. The conversation was emotional. A woman in our church had a crisis, and she needed me immediately. I weighed the situation and thought this "crisis" was more chronic than acute, and less immediate than the caller said. I told her I would come later because I had an appointment for the next couple of hours. I prayed for her and said I would come over when I finished the appointment.

I looked at my daughter's face, and it relayed a new message to me. This time her face said, "I am important." We went for our trail ride. When I came back, I put the horses out in the field, cleaned the tack, and put it away. I phoned the woman who had called earlier, and she was much calmer. She told me God had intervened; her situation was under control, and I need not come over. She thanked me for my prayers.

This experience marked a positive turning point in my relationship with my daughter. Church leaders must schedule uninterrupted time off with family. Some crises must be looked after, but they occur far less often than we realize.

A similar situation happened in the same church. A pastor and his wife from a downtown Vancouver, BC, church stayed at our home for a few days. The phone rang during coffee late one morning on my day off. I answered it, hung up, and said to our visitors, "I must go into town for a few minutes." They asked why. I explained that a couple had moved to the island but had no money and no place to stay. They came over on the ferry and brought nothing with them.

My pastor friend asked me what I going to do. I said, "I'll get them some groceries, book a motel room for a few nights,

> I said, "Right, that's what I do. I am a pastor and I care for people."

and help them find work." He said, "Why are you being so stupid?" I was offended by what he said and asked him to explain. He said, "These two people came over here to live on the island, they brought nothing with them, and you are going to meet their every need?"

I said, "Right, that's what I do. I am a pastor and I care for people." He used the word stupid again in describing my plan. He explained that these two people came here with a problem and offered it to me, and I took it immediately and made it own.

He said, "This is not your problem, it's their problem." His advice was to meet them, tell them that I would be happy to get them something to eat, and pay their ferry fare back to the mainland. He said to tell them that it would be fine for them to move to the island but only when they meet their financial needs or find a job. I was upset because I had been found out. I was playing the Messiah by meeting people's needs. Of course God received the glory, but I had taken his place in many people's lives. I went to town and did what my friend said. My ministry changed that day and my stress level lessened considerably. I was now a facilitator for God rather than a messiah, and this lowered the risk of compassion fatigue.

The Messiah Trap

Pastors and other church leaders may fall into the messiah trap because they are "called to minister." The pastoral call motivates them to offer all they have and all they are to those they serve. In *When Helping You Is Hurting Me,*

Carman Renee Berry suggests many church leaders struggle with the messiah syndrome. She describes the syndrome as a two-sided coin. One side says, "If I don't do what is needed, it won't get done," and the opposite side of coin says, "Everyone else's needs are more important than mine."[128]

This problem surfaces with pastors who believe they must give all and care for those God entrusts to them. The idea of "being poured out as a drink offering to the Lord" (Phil. 2:17) has potential power over pastors. Guilt motivates church leaders who neglect self-care and experience the messiah syndrome. The result is the loss of emotion, empathy, and compassion. Messianic pastors can't help anyone, including themselves. The guilt feeling for failing God and not meeting everyone's needs can be overwhelming.

Guilt, Shame, and Depression: Residual Effects of Dysfunction

I realized I come from a dysfunctional home when I took my first seminary counseling course. My professor asked our class how many had been in police work, ambulance service, fire department, or search and rescue either full-time or part-time. Forty-five students raised their hands in a class of fifty. I discovered many people come from dysfunctional homes are rescuers. If you didn't come from a dysfunctional home you missed thinking that pain, misery, and low self-esteem were normal. Of course no one is normal. Normal is a setting on a dryer.

For a while I believed my life must be normally dys-functional because everyone I knew had similar feelings and experience. If you find the word "dysfunction" in the dictionary, perhaps your family history illustrates it. My dys-function may originate from my mother's mixed messages. One night she worked late and came home, expecting I was sound asleep. I wasn't in bed because I had snuck out and placed on my pillow a white styrofoam wig stand with hand-drawn sleeping eyes. The white head and the moonlight made it look like a corpse. My mother thought I died in my sleep and was really upset, but more upset when she found out I wasn't in bed. She was angry and said she wanted to kill me. Mixed messages of love can cause dysfunction.

I also learned that our emotions are shaped or suppressed during our childhood. My dysfunction was forced upon me. I lost my Dad to cancer before I became a teen-ager. Five years of suffering, fear, anger, and confusion for him and our family preceded his death. I drank alcohol to numb the pain and release my feelings. As I recall my teens and early twenties, I got angry over the smallest thing. I was lonely, hurt, and almost sure no one cared about me or how I felt. I know now that this wasn't true, but at the time I believed it.

I chose a welding career for a stable income in a recognized occupation that would raise my family's economic standard. I knew welding would be a secure occupation, but most of my co-workers liked to drink and party. I joined the volunteer fire department and ambulance crew shortly after becoming a welder. I realize the social aspect drew me to this organization.

I also wanted to help others and lessen their pain or discomfort. A counselor might suggest I was a rescuer. The fire department and ambulance calls became more interesting

> I also wanted to help others and lessen others' pain or discomfort.

and exciting, and I soon left welding. I became a full-time ambulance attendant. I helped many people in crises, and this career became a springboard to what I really desired. After five years, I left my ambulance career and became a counselor and pastor for victims of dysfunctional family systems. I now counsel and care for victims of sexual abuse who were filled with anger, living in fear, and addicted to alcohol and drugs. I believed my upbringing gave me insight and helped me relate.

If life hands you a lemon, make lemonade out of it, but I found I couldn't make lemonade out of the lemon alone. I needed someone who could give me life, and Jesus was that someone. Jesus said, "The thief comes to steal, kill and destroy; I came that you might have life and that life more abundantly." (John 10:10). I am not completely functional yet and have never claimed to be normal, but I have come a long way. I enjoy life abundantly. We can take the place of our Messiah Jesus and become lemonade makers for others, but it's unhealthy. We deplete our compassion reserves and become compassion fatigued.

Guilt is a feeling I have done something wrong. Another way to see this is to view our lives as vehicles that travel through life. Guilt is the fuel supply for persons from dysfunctional families, and powers our drive along the road of life. Shame is the windshield through which we view the passing world, and depression is the darkness that envelops what we see through the windshield of shame. The weight of guilt and shame can sink church leaders into

> Shame is the windshield through which we view the passing world.

depression even though they believe in God's power to set captives free and heal sickness and disease. Grant Mullen describes the journey into depression and the effects this downward spiral may have on Christians:

> Depressed Christians feel like hypocrites for not being able to pray, worship or read the Bible. . . . Unfortunately this inability to pray and study will indicate to the friends that the depressed person must have a spiritual problem, be living in sin, have a lack of faith or that they really don't want to get well. . . . You can see then that the depressed Christian not only suffers the symptoms of the mood disorder but they also carry the guilt and shame put upon them by other Christians who don't understand the condition. Non-Christians don't have to endure this added burden so that's why Christians have more pain from depression than non-believers.[129]

We Are Created in the Image of God

An unbalanced lifestyle affects the health and wellbeing of spirit, soul, and body. Church leaders often focus on developing others' spiritual lives and ministering to them, but neglect the body and soul. The Creator shaped spirit, soul, and body together to function in perfect balance. When one segment becomes unbalanced, the whole person loses equilibrium and spins out of control. The results can be disastrous, but discipline, meditation, physical exercise, proper nutrition, adequate sleep, Sabbath observance and humor offer are solutions and prevent compassion fatigue.

Life in Balance

Balance is a delicate dance for most people, especially church leaders. Persons' whole beings are involved when they respond to God's call to serve others. They focus their lives on fulfilling this call. In the process, spiritual caregivers may fall into the compassion fatigue trap and experience physical sickness, emotional depletion, or spiritual emptiness. This physical, emotional, and spiritual damage unbalances caregivers. I have two questions: What are the components of a Christ-centered, balanced life? Why do church leaders neglect solutions to unbalanced lives?

Paul underscored the triune composition of human beings, "May God himself, the God who makes everything holy and whole, make you holy and whole, put you

> May the God who makes everything holy and whole, make you holy and whole, put you together—spirit, soul, and body.

together—spirit, soul, and body—and keep you fit for the

coming of our Master, Jesus Christ. The One who called you is completely dependable. If he said it, he'll do it." (1 Thess. 5:23).[130] Paul's words resonate with church leaders. Paul confirms that God put us together, called us, and desires to keep us in balance for Christ's return. Paul says Jesus isers church leaders balanced lives.

"Steadiness" and "stability" also describe balance. A three-legged stool depicts balance and stability as Walter Whitely explains:

> First imagine trying to place a two-legged stool on the floor. The stool will, essentially, pivot about the line joining those two points of contact. It will not be stable. However, any third leg (of a reasonable length) will contact the floor at exactly one of the positions as it pivots about the line. When it does, that will be what you call the "steady" position. The top of the stool may not be parallel to the floor but the stool will be in a stable position. The stable position is robust in terms of small errors in the lengths of the legs or the flatness of the floor.[131]

This metaphor describes our triune composition. One leg represents the spirit, the second leg represents the soul, and the third leg represents the body. Church leaders experience balance and stability in their lives when their spirits, souls, and bodies synchronize. The *Merriam-Webster Dictionary* defines balance as a state of "mental and emotional steadiness."[132] Balance prevents compassion fatigue.

The three-legged stool's stability and usefulness depend on legs of approximately the same length. The stool remains stable even if one leg is shorter; however, the seat's usefulness may be compromised if its angle is severe. A balanced life involves spirit, soul, and body. If leaders neglect any of these areas, they will experience unbalanced, unhealthy lives. Leaders tend to adjust the seat and do not lengthen or strengthen the compromised leg. Leaders may make unhealthy choices such as workaholism, materialism, extra marital affairs, pornography, overspending, or the use of drugs or alcohol to adjust the seat.

Their unhealthy decisions may cause depression, anger, burnout, or compassion fatigue. Church leaders may experience spiritual sinkholes due to the subtle erosion of their balanced lives. Continued imbalance may cause serious spiritual, psychological, and physiological problems, and compassion fatigue results. Rob Bell writes about the stress of success that depleted his compassion and opened a large emotional sinkhole in his life:

We were growing. House churches were springing up, partnerships were beginning with other churches around the world, and people who had never been a part of a church were finding a home. Two years into it, around 10,000 people were coming to three gatherings on Sundays. In the middle of all this chaos was me, super pastor, doing weddings and funerals and giving spiritual direction and going to meetings and teaching and dealing with crises and visiting people in prison and at the hospital. . . . I escaped to the storage closet to be alone. I was moments away from leaving the whole thing; I just couldn't do it anymore.[133]

What Is the Problem Here?

The postmodern movement may be a source of our busyness and Sabbath rest neglect, but pastors bare responsibility for losing touch with God's call to shepherd the flock. Perhaps the ancient image of the shepherd who leads sheep by still waters and makes them lie down in green grass no longer applies. Perhaps the contemporary image is a church leader who runs on a spiritual autobahn and leads tired, thirsty sheep who eat spiritual fast food, attempt too many things, and move at breakneck speed. This pace is self-inflicted by church leaders who fail to recognize their ministerial roles. They should recognize that they serve because of God, not as substitutes for God.

In *Working the Angles,* Eugene Peterson uses a different metaphor to describe contemporary pastoral ministry busyness:

> The pastors of America have metamorphosed into a company of shopkeepers, and the shops they keep are churches. They are occupied with shopkeepers concerns—how to keep the customers happy, how to lure customers away from the competitors down the street, how to package the goods so that customers will lay out more money. Some of them are very good shopkeepers. They attract a lot of customers, pull in great sums of money, and develop splendid reputations. Yet it is still shop keeping, religious shop keeping to be sure, but shop keeping all the same. The marketing strategies of the fast-food franchise occupy the waking minds of the entrepreneurs; while asleep they dream of the kind of success that will get the attention of journalists.[134]

Excessive busyness without Sabbath rest creates compassion fatigue.

Balancing Three Legs: Spirit, Soul, and Body

Mary Oliver challenges readers to live balanced lifestyles in her poem, *The Summer Day*, "Tell me, what

> "Tell me, what is it you plan to do with your one wild and precious life?"

is it you plan to do with your one wild and precious life?"[135]
The use of words 'wild' and 'precious' challenges readers to
enjoy a wild life, full of excitement while respecting life as
precious. This is possible when three; equally healthy legs
support the stool: spirit, soul,
and body. A well-balanced
life avoids compassion
fatigue.

> Jesus took time away for refreshment and reju-venation, but he did not live a monastic life.

The First Leg: Spirit

Humanity desires spiritual experiences. This desire
reflects our nature and is essential to health and balance in
church leaders' lives. Followers of Christ have sought to
develop their spirits through the centuries, For example,
twelfth century Benedict of Aniane sought spiritual development through European monasteries. He isolated the monasteries and focused the monks' attention on the *opus Dei*,[136]
the work of God and prayer. Hoyt and Chodorow write:

> The new monks made the inner person their principal
> concern and sought to explore the ways . . . a person
> can achieve the level of spiritual awareness neces-
> sary for knowledge (that is, experience) of God. On
> the one hand, this mystical interest produced works
> of deep psychological analysis and insight. On the

182

other hand, monastic theology became experiential, designed to raise the mind to a higher spiritual level.[137]

I believe this exemplifies an unbalanced spiritual life. Cloistering and seeking disciplined spiritually may produce religious experience but doesn't promote ministry with the unconverted, and it differs from Jesus' model for church leaders. Jesus took time for refreshment and rejuvenation, but he did not live a monastic life. Scripture provides a more balanced approach for spiritual development.

Dallas Willard suggests we create a list of disciplines to strengthen the spiritual component of our lives:

> In shaping our own list of spiritual disciplines, we should keep in mind that very few disciplines can be regarded as absolutely indispensable for healthy spiritual life and work, though some are obviously more important than others. Practicing a range of activities that have proven track records across centuries will keep us from erring. And, if later, other activities are really more what we need, our progress won't be seriously hindered, and we'll probably be led to them.[138]

Willard suggests believers pursue the disciplines our cloistered brothers and sisters practiced, but in a balanced fashion. The goal is integration of the spiritual disciplines into daily actions that strengthen our spirits. The disciplines are "solitude, silence, fasting, frugality, chastity, secrecy, sacrifice, study, worship, celebration, service, prayer, fellowship, confession, and submission."[139] Leaders who incorporate these disciplines into their lives balance and strengthen their spirits. Three disciplines are important to the spiritual formation process of Christian leaders: solitude, worship, and prayer.

Solitude

Solitude is a rare commodity in our fast-paced, competitive world. Willard believes solitude separates us from distractions that compete for our attention and allows us to confront our souls.[140] In solitude we cling to Christ, are refreshed, and return to society as freed captives. Louis Bouyer describes solitude as isolation and reflection, "Solitude is a terrible trial, for it serves to crack open and burst apart the shell of our superficial securities. It opens out to us the unknown abyss that we all carry within us . . . [and] discloses the fact that these abysses are haunted."[141] God designed Sabbath to take us away from life's busyness so we can contemplate and meditate on our inner selves. Willard believes our observance of this discipline frees our spirits, and we can return renewed and refreshed to home, job, community, and church.[142] Solitude is an antidote to compassion fatigue.

Worship

Worship is more than music, more than singing hymns, more than contemporary choruses in a Sunday morning church service. Willard describes worship as an act that "we engage ourselves with, dwell upon, and express the greatness, beauty, and goodness of God through thought and the use of words, rituals, and symbols. We do this alone, as well as in union with God's people. To worship is to see God as worthy, to ascribe great worth to him."[143] Believers worship God with their whole being, the human spirit unites with the Spirit of God, and a mystical intimacy occurs between Creator and creature.

Edward J. Farrell describes worship and the adoration of God. He believes the impact of adoration has been dimmed or lost, and contemporary people are uncertain what it means: "We 'adore' many things—the word is in common use, is used to describe lesser and often inane things or ideas. Thus 'adoration' in its religious and original sense—the bowing down in awe and the reverence, tinged with the fear of God—has become largely lost in superficial wonder and feeling."[144] Farrell identifies how the loss of adoration's meaning affects the contemporary church. Worship discipline focused on Jesus Christ can refresh our understanding and lead God's followers to worship him intimately.

Bob Sorge describes worship as "our affirmative response to the self-revelation of the triune God. For the Christian leader each act of life is an act of worship when it is done with love that responds to the Father's love. Living should be constant worshiping, since worship may be said to provide the metabolism for spiritual life."[145] Worship provides metabolism for spiritual life, and followers of Christ should develop this daily discipline. The results are freedom and rejuvenation, which are antidotes to compassion fatigue.

Prayer

Leaders trust God, develop faith, and recognize God's voice through prayer. Prayer is simple and practiced easily anywhere, any time, but is often neglected. Thomas Merton shares his thoughts prayer, "There is a 'movement' of mediation, expressing the basic 'paschal' rhythm of the Christian life, the passage from death to life in Christ. Sometimes prayer, meditation and contemplation are 'death' — a kind helplessness, frustration, infidelity, confusion, and ignorance."[146]

Merton describes prayer as a death to self, busyness, time constraints, and egocentricity. This death produces intimate conversations with God; the one who prays becomes a listener. The discipline of prayer can lead to development, strength, correction, and avoidance of compassion fatigue. The idea is development of the inner spirit.

The Second Leg: The Soul

The soul concept is fascinating, and some have attempted to weigh the soul upon death, hoping to determine its supposed mass. For example, a Christian named Duncan MacDougall, a self-proclaimed physician, attempted to do that in 1907. His research came under much scrutiny, was later declared unscientific, and his findings were found false. He estimated the soul's weight at twenty-one grams.[147]

I believe the soul is affected by environmental stress, and stress invades twenty-first century life. Heart disease is on the rise and medical conditions like burnout, compassion fatigue, and emotional exhaustion are household words. Many of these conditions relate to the increase of stress in North American culture.

Sally Helegsen offers a historical perspective about workplace stress. She describes the large, permanently located machinery of the industrial era that requires workers to travel to the factory. Many North Americans use small portable tools for 'knowledge work' and many people can work anywhere and all the time. Helgesen suggests work was easier to manage and less stressful before the industrial revolution:

> Indeed, we are living in greater intimacy with our work today than people in the pre-industrial era, when most of the work was done on the farm, at the manor house, or in the cottage. In that world, however, longstanding traditions and religious observance, often tied to the changing of the seasons, as well as the impossibility of working after dark, prevented work from taking over people's lives. None of these barriers protect us today.[148]

Many Christian leaders adopt demanding business models and technology for church growth and operations, and churches serve busy twenty-first century people. As a result, church leaders exhibit symptoms of stress diseases, similar to their secular counterparts—compassion fatigue results. The soul processes stress. Watchman Nee suggests that the soul is where body and spirit merge, making it the site of personality and influence. Nee writes, "[T]he soul is the site of personality. The will, intellect, and emotions are there."[149] If we accept this definition of the soul, we understand why people are constantly under attack and susceptible to stress and compassion fatigue. Church leaders are not exempt. The soul has three components: emotion, intellect, and the will. They are susceptible to stress and compassion fatigue.

Emotions

Church leaders run the gamut of emotions daily. The morning could start off as a peaceful time of mediation and an emotional/spiritual connection with God; however, the car might not start, and you might be late for a meeting. Add to this a call from the

> Church leaders run the gamut of emotions daily.

hospital from the new church couple that had a baby and want you to visit. The next few hours might include a funeral for a member of your church's youth group, a boy who took his own life. Time is tight because you have a wedding an hour after the funeral, and it will take thirty minutes to drive to the location if the traffic is light. The evening is similar. The church board meets, and finances are low. As a leader, you must make difficult decisions about staff downsizing and the future of missions and church programs.

This scenario is extreme, but it describes stressors found in daily pastoral work that affect your emotional stability. Personal stressors also affect every leader's life: finances, marriage relationships,

> It is important to remain a lifelong learner and deliver information that you are comfortable offering.

family relationships, aging parents, and unresolved personal baggage. The soul becomes a target for many emotions, often felt simultaneously.

In *The Emotional Brain*, Joseph LeDoux contends that the brain processes emotions, and persons choose their responses to stressors. Effective church leaders must cultivate healthy emotional systems, because leaders may make wrong choices in the face of stressors sent to a burdened, tired brain. This condition may also lead to compassion fatigue and depression.

Intellect

In addition to emotions, the soul involves the intellect, and intellect is critical to church leaders. Church leaders learn formally through education and informally through life experiences, and well-informed church leaders serve more effectively. Their knowledge gives them confidence about what they offer persons in need. The opposite is also true. Lack of knowledge may create feelings of inadequacy and lack of confidence.

In this era of lightening quick information access, many leaders feel overwhelmed by the amount of knowledge required to meet congregational needs. It is important to remain a lifelong learner and deliver information that you are comfortable offering.

The Will

The will is the third part of the soul, and it is critical to the decision process carried out by emotion and intellect. Nee writes, "Our emotion merely express how we feel; our mind simply tells us what we think, but our will communicates what we want. Hence it is the most influential component of our entire person."[150]

The will draws from previous experience, personal desire, and a predetermined value system. Unregenerate persons may choose selfish, hedonistic, self-gratifying, and possibly sadistic behavior towards others and self. On the other hand, Christians' wills unite with God's will through salvation and regeneration in Jesus Christ. Paul writes, "Therefore, if anyone is in Christ, he is a new creation; the old has gone, the new has come." (2 Cor. 5:17). Paul reiterates this theme, "Do not conform any longer to the pattern of this world, but be transformed by the renewing of your mind. Then you will be able to test and approve what God's will is—his good, pleasing and perfect will." (Rom. 12:2).

Stanley Grenz believes regenerate Christians can choose to live in synchrony with God's will:

> Not only is God's law written on the human heart, but, more important, the indwelling Spirit mediates divine revelation directly to each believer. As a consequence of the Spirit's internal presence, advocates add, the ethical life flows quite naturally out of our inner being, which is the location of the Spirit. The indwelling Spirit renews and sanctifies our moral consciousness, mediating to us an intuitive sense of the right and the good.[151]

Our ability to choose gives us freedom that leads to destructive behavior if influenced negatively. Human will is a powerful force and God does not overrule his creation's choices. We choose right or wrong.

Spirits and souls jointly influence leaders' choices. Multiple factors influence choices we make: faith or its absence, a balanced lifestyle or addictive behavior, new and residual stress, and our coping capacities. Some leaders make choices that can deplete emotional reserves and cause compassion fatigue. The body is the third leg of the stool.

> Human will is a powerful force and God does not overrule his creation's choices.

The Third Leg: The Body

The well maintained spirit and soul are two thirds of the healthy lifestyle equation that avoids compassion fatigue. The body is third component. A well rested, exercised and fed body completes a balanced lifestyle. The body is more than the vehicle that

> I left the graveyard. My chest pain intensified and radiated into my jaw and down my left arm.

transports the spirit and the soul; it demands machine-like maintenance.

A large waistline and cyclic chest pain under stress attest to my difficulty with self-discipline and self-denial. I officiated on one of my days off at a graveside committal for a man from our congregation

> Church leaders are like spiritual ironman competitors who enter triathlons of spiritual endurance.

who died of cancer at the age of thirty-eight. I stood beside that open grave and said comforting words to the grieving family and friends. As I spoke, I experienced excruciating chest pain. I looked away from family and scanned the open area of the graveyard. I looked for a plot for myself because I thought I was having a heart attack. I said nothing and spared the grieving family and friends.

I left the graveyard. My chest pain intensified and radiated into my jaw and down my left arm. These are classic signs of serious cardiac distress. I told the grieving family that I would be at the reception in about an hour and left with my wife, but first I had to make a hospital visit. A young couple in our church had a new baby. As I sat in the maternity ward, the pain intensified. I excused myself and went the Emergency Ward to see a physician. I relayed my symptoms. The physician calculated my age, asked the duration and location of the pain, placed me on a stretcher, ran some tests, and attached cardiac monitors.

I asked someone to tell my wife that I was being admitted to the hospital. The tests revealed no cardiac problems; stress caused my chest pain. The physician told me I had a choice. I must time off immediately and rest or I might suffer a heart attack. The physician said I could spend the next four days in the cardiac observation unit where I would do nothing stressful and medications would relax me. Or, I could take my family away, spend four days in a hotel watching TV, swimming, and eating popcorn. I chose the trip, hotel, swimming, and popcorn.

The physician also suggested I develop an exercise program and change my eating habits. I did well for the first few months, but then my desire to walk every night waned. One windy, rainy night I justified not walking because of the weather, but these words came to mind, "It rains and the wind blows outside the window of the Intensive Care Ward of the hospital. Would you rather be inside during those evenings or outside enduring a little weather?" I walked. The body needs exercise and a proper diet.

Exercise

Regular exercise is critical to stress management. The physiological benefits of exercise are instantaneous, and a healthy, well-maintained body meets stress situations with less wear and tear and avoids compassion fatigue. Church leaders are like spiritual ironman competitors who enter triathlons of spiritual endurance. Joe Friel and Gordon Byrn use this metaphor and advise church leaders about maintaining endurance. They base their advice on common sense: eat properly, maintain fluid levels, race smart, and pace yourself. The authors say, "You can practice your ability to focus during any workout—hard, easy, long, or short. It is a critical success factor for having a solid race."[152] Like disciplined athletes, church leaders should observe the practical, everyday needs essential to their bodies' well being. Friel and Byrn's statement could be modified for church leaders, "Focus is a critical success factor for a good, solid, healthy ministry."

Diet

The body needs fuel like any machine, and like poor grades of gasoline or contaminated fuels, the wrong food interferes with the body's potential performance. Kenford Nedd describes how food becomes fuel in our bodies. He says what we eat, when we eat, and how we affect our ability to deal with stress. He describes the physiological effects of fat, sugar, carbohydrates, and protein on the body and emotions.

Sugar must be balanced by an insulin increase and this causes irritability, nervousness, and hunger. Adrenaline and cortisol spike in the bloodstream, which raises the blood sugar again, and the cycle repeats, "until your body wears itself out."[153] Persons under stress who choose proper diets as a routine discipline add longevity and lead healthier lives. The combination of exercise and a proper diet allows the body to function at its best in all circumstances, maintain strength and power, aid heal and restoration, and avoid compassion fatigue.

Balance through Reflection

Healthy spirits, souls, and bodies work together in harmony and discipline to affect a balanced lifestyle and avoid stress-related illnesses and compassion fatigue. This is easier said than done. The benefits of balance are health, strength, and clear thinking. Balance allows church leaders to endure the difficult challenges of ministry, recover quickly, and enjoy restful and relaxing times that rejuvenate the spirit, soul and body and strengthen them for ministry. Leaders who develop balanced lifestyles monitor their bodies and know when they need rest and repair. Church leaders who develop a balance of rest and work will lessen the risk of compassion fatigue. Sharon Promislow offers a plan for a balanced life:

> If we want to help our body attain and maintain a state of emotional, physical, and mental wellbeing, it makes sense for us to do all of the following: moderate the stressors in our lives, eat right, sleep right, manage our time, exercise, and do brain/body balancers designed to give our system a chance to naturally manufacture the appropriate biochemicals necessary for a balanced state[154]

The three-legged stool is a great picture of stability, and Promislow's method makes it possible to balance securely on the stool aware of the variability of the seat's angle and make necessary adjustments.

Shabbat
Relax and Re-Create

Do you find yourself filling the Messiah's role in your ministry?

The idea of "being poured out as a drink offering to the Lord" has power over church leaders. How does it affect your ministry?

The balance of life is a delicate dance for most people. Who leads in your life?

When life becomes unbalanced, church leaders may make unhealthy choices: workaholism, materialism, extra marital affairs, pornography, over-spending, use of drugs or alcohol. Are you involved in an unhealthy choice? If so, ask for forgiveness and seek counsel.

The ancient image of the shepherd who leads sheep by still waters and makes them lie down in green grass no longer applies. Perhaps the contemporary image is a church leader who runs on a spiritual autobahn and leads tired, thirsty sheep who eat spiritual fast food, attempt too many things, and move at breakneck speed. How does your life compare to this statement?

Reflect on your spiritual disciplines. Are you faithful to your personal growth and relationship to Christ?

Reflect on your physical disciplines. Do you have an exercise program and eat a proper diet? If not, set up a program at a local gym and be accountable to someone for your exercise and your diet.

CONCLUSION

S tress in the twenty-first century is rampant in spite of time and energy saving devices. Progress generates stress. Our society runs at full-speed, and many couples work two jobs, place their children in daycare, and commute long distances. Adult children must help elderly parents make decisions about retirement homes, care homes, and the possibility of three generations living together. The media relays horrific trauma, global terrorism, and frequent and heinous local crimes during the dinner hour and evening through our televisions, computers, and Blackberries. These stresses drain our emotions, energy, and strength, and we feel empty. This subtle erosion creates sinkholes and leads to compassion fatigue.

Erosion is subtle and unseen until it removes underlying supports and undercuts the pavement that carries a vehicle's weight. The collapse is inevitable when erosion accomplishes its work. Nothing is left to support the asphalt's weight, and the surface collapses and causes serious damage to the road structure. The sinkhole analogy describes compassion fatigue. Stress undercuts church leaders' emotional, physical, and spiritual strength, and they collapse under pressure and experience compassion fatigue.

Pastors, counselors and other care giving church leaders young and old, fall victim to compassion fatigue, a serious condition common among caregivers in all fields.

Pastors and church leaders experience increased stress. Pastors serve congregational members, conduct weddings and funerals, make hospital visits and court related appearances, counsel victims of childhood sexual abuse and clergy who act immorally. How can pastors function under these demands and pressures in their everyday lives? It is imperative that church leaders understand the signs and symptoms of compassion fatigue to avoid personal destruction.

The pressures of success, materialism, job security, and time management have replaced the gentle peace and rest available in the Lord's presence. Our North American culture is driven by success and has pulled the church into its web. Pastors and leaders strive to prove their spiritual success measured by church growth, new buildings, and increased budgets. Many called by God never achieve these goals because they use up their resources, do not take the time to refill, and neglect Sabbath rest. Some encounter sinkholes and the results are often tragic. The fall is a result of stress and the emotional and psychological depletion caused by a lack of Sabbath rest. The thin outside covering caves in under pressure from the need and demand of others.

Life requires balance. God gave his followers a proven prescription for avoiding compassion fatigue. This prescription is found in the fourth of the Ten Commandments. Longevity and peak performance happen in ministry when church leaders follow balanced lifestyles that include a biblical cycle of Sabbath rest and preventive maintenance. Lack of rest is a key component in the rapid onset of compassion fatigue among Christian leaders. Ironically, these same leaders use the fourth commandment to counsel others but do not apply it to their own busy lives.

Church leaders can jump off the busyness treadmill and become Sabbath observers who are rested and re-created in Christ. Neglect of Sabbath is sinful disobedience. The writer of Hebrews states, "Let us, therefore, be diligent to enter that same rest, lest anyone fall through following the same example of disobedience." (Heb. 4:11). We neglect God's invitation and command when we are too busy doing God's work and fail to enter into his presence. Church leaders may experience a paradox because they are called to minister consistently for God and enjoy Sabbath rest. Hebrews 4:9-10 provides a resolution, "There remains therefore a Sabbath rest for the people of God. For one who has entered his rest has himself also rested from his works, as God did from his."

When church leaders neglect Sabbath rest, the Holy Spirit cannot minister through them completely. They may undertake ministry in their own strength because they lack faith that God will complete his work through them. Lack of trust is lack of faith, which is sin, "Whatever is not from faith, is sin." (Rom. 14:23c). The Holy Spirit offers church leaders strength and power to accomplish God's plans through an environment of faith and rest. Sabbath rest is not idleness; it is stress-less productivity.

Jesus taught his followers that Sabbath legalism brought bondage and death. Jesus modeled correct Sabbath observance when he separated from the crowds' demands and worldly busyness and spent time in his Father's presence. When Jesus realized his followers intended to make him king by force, he withdrew to the mountain alone (John 6:15).

Pastors and church leaders run the rat race. Pastors know the fourth commandment that God etched on granite with his own finger, and they understand his instructions about healthy, productive living. Like Moses, however, they often fail to observe God's prescription for rest. They mentor congregations of busy people with families, careers, eldercare. People seek rest. Perhaps time will be the most sought after currency in the future, not money or possessions. Time is in short supply and lack of time creates lack of rest.

Weddings or funerals happen often on pastors' personal Sabbath days. They may take another day off, but it often becomes another day of ministry. Pagers and cell phones are barriers to pastoral Sabbaths. Pastors remain connected on days off or at retreats, and they can be summoned at a moment's notice. Cell phones are technological shackles that keep our central nervous systems on constant alert. It is difficult for pastors' bodies and minds to rest and experience Sabbath as God intended.

Sabbath rest is more than a day off, an annual vacation, or a life separated from the world. This is especially true if we feel guilty about not doing something, or doing things that were not completed in the other six days. God planned that our lifetimes include *shabbat* or Sabbath rest. Life should be a cycle of work and rest, not work, work, work, and then rest. God did not plan that his creatures labor for years without rest and then cease work and enter into eternal rest. The Creator gives directions for life for his creation, including those called to lead his church.

Pastoral ministry is about caring. God calls pastors to shepherd others, and he brings them into intimate, caring proximity with people entrusted to their care. On many occasions, God uses church leaders to help others grow and mature in his love. Compassionate church leaders create environments of comfort and support, and help alleviate others' pain and suffering. God equips spiritual caregivers and calls them to be his love in action, but this privilege comes at a high cost and may empty the shepherd leaders' compassion reserves. Leaders may not replenish their compassion reserves through times of refreshment and re-creation in the Lord's presence.

The words spoken by pastors and church leaders during difficult times have two layers. One layer is God's love, and the other is pastors' compassion. Church leaders often give themselves in emotionally-charged situations. If they do not constantly refill and refresh themselves, they deplete their compassion reserves and will be ineffective in ministry and their own lives.

Suffering extracts compassion from those created in God's image and sensitive to his Holy Spirit. This is a good and troubling notion. It is good because sufferers have compassionate pastoral companions during painful journeys. It is troubling because compassionate companions witness and feel victims' torments and fears. Compassionate people hurt when others hurt, and empathic pastors suffer with those on the journey. God accompanies suffering travelers, and pastors must know when to stop at rest areas. We must take time for re-creation, then catch up to Jesus and rejoin those who suffer.

Recognizing the condition of compassion fatigue is crucial, and equally important is the knowledge that there is help for those who suffer from it. I think pastoral leaders must answer a difficult question, "Why don't we care for ourselves as much as we care for others?" Self care is essential for church leaders who seek longevity in ministry and a healthy personal life with family and friends.

An unbalanced, un-rested lifestyle affects the health and wellbeing of spirit, soul, and body. Church leaders often develop others' spiritual lives and minister to them, but neglect their own bodies and souls. The Creator shaped spirit, soul, and body together to function in perfect balance. When one segment becomes unbalanced, the whole person loses equilibrium and spins out of control, and the results can be disastrous. Discipline, meditation, physical exercise, proper nutrition, adequate sleep, and Sabbath observance are solutions and prevent compassion fatigue.

Balance is a delicate dance for most people, including church leaders. Persons' whole beings are involved when they respond to God's call to serve others, and they focus their lives on fulfilling this call. In the process, spiritual caregivers may fall into the compassion fatigue sinkhole and experience physical sickness, emotional depletion, or spiritual emptiness. This physical, emotional, and spiritual damage unbalances caregivers.

We desire spiritual experiences. This desire reflects our nature and is essential to health and balance. Sabbath solitude is a rare commodity in our fast-paced, competitive world. In solitude we cling to Christ, are refreshed, and return to society as freed persons. Solitude is an antidote to compassion fatigue. Believers worship God with their whole being, the human spirit unites with the Spirit of God, and a mystical intimacy occurs between Creator and creature. Sabbath worship provides metabolism for spiritual life, and followers of Christ should develop this daily discipline. The results are freedom and rejuvenation that are antidotes to compassion fatigue. Leaders trust God, develop faith, and recognize God's voice through prayer. Prayer is simple and practiced easily anywhere, any time, but it is often neglected.

A well rested, exercised and fed body completes a balanced lifestyle. The body is more than the vehicle that transports the spirit and the soul; it requires machine-like maintenance. Regular exercise is critical to stress management. The physiological benefits of exercise are instantaneous, and a healthy, well-maintained body meets stress situations with less wear and tear and avoids compassion fatigue.

The body needs fuel like any machine, and like poor grades of gasoline or contaminated fuels, the wrong food interferes with the body's performance. Persons under stress who choose proper diets as a routine discipline add longevity and lead healthier lives. Together exercise and a proper diet allow the body to function at its best in all circumstances, maintain strength and power, aid healing and restoration, and avoid compassion fatigue.

Healthy spirits, souls, and bodies work in harmony and discipline through balanced lifestyles that avoid stress-related illnesses and compassion fatigue. The benefits are health, strength, and clear thinking. Balance allows church leaders to endure the difficult challenges of ministry, recover quickly, and enjoy restful and relaxing times that rejuvenate the spirit, soul and body for ministry.

Leaders who develop balanced lifestyles monitor their bodies and know when they need rest and repair. Church leaders who develop a balance of Sabbath rest and healthy habits can avoid compassion fatigue.

ENDNOTES

Introduction

1. John Swigert Jr., James Lovell, and Fred Haise Jr., made up the Apollo 13 crew. They used a similar phrase to report a major technical problem to the Houston base, http://www. phrases.org.uk/ meanings/188425.html (accessed on August 29, 2008).

2. James Dobson. "The Titanic. The Church. What They Have in Common," http://www2.focusonthefamily.com/ docstudy/newsletters/A000000803.cfm (accessed January 25, 2010)

3. Jeffery T. Mitchell, "Basic Critical Incident Stress Management," (course notes, Courtney Fire Department, Courtney, BC, December 4-5, 2003).

4. Hans Selye, *The Stress of Life* (New York: McGraw Hill, 1976).

5. Mitchell, "Basic Critical Incident Stress Management," (course notes, Courtney Fire Department, Courtney, BC, December 4-5, 2003).

6. ibid.

7. Charles F. Figley, "Traumatization and Comfort: Close Relationships May Be Hazardous to Your Health," (keynote presentation at the Conference on Families and Close Relationships: Individuals in Social Interaction, Texas Tech University, Lubbock, TX, 1982).

8. Charles F. Figley, *Compassion Fatigue: Coping with Secondary Traumatic Stress Disorder in Those Who Treat the Traumatized* (Bristol, PA: Brunner/Mazel, 1995), 1.

CHAPTER ONE

9. Jim Lanier, "Take Care of Yourself," *The Journal of Emergency Dispatch* 10, no.4 (July/August, 2008): 23-28.

10. Charles Figley, "Compassion Fatigue: Toward a New Understanding of the Cost of Caring," in *Secondary Traumatic Stress: Self-Care Issues for Clinicians, Researchers, and Educators,* ed. B. Hudnall Stamm (Baltimore, MD: Sidran Press, 1999), 4.

11. Gordon, MacDonald, *Ordering Your Private World* (Nashville, TN: Thomas Nelson, 1985), 15.

12. Casting Crowns Album: Love Them Like Jesus, http://www.christianrocklyrics.com/ castingcrowns/lovethem-likejesus.php (accessed March 19, 2007).

13. Nicolas Woltterstorff, *Lament for a Son* (Grand Rapids, MI: William B. Eerdmans, 1987), 34.

14. Eugene H. Peterson, *Five Smooth Stones for Pastoral Work* (Grand Rapids, MI: William B. Eerdmans, 1980), 126.

15. Ibid., 135.

16. Ibid., 136.

17. Charles Figley, the founding father of compassion fatigue research, coined this phrase. Figley. *Compassion Fatigue: Coping with Secondary Traumatic Stress Disorder in Those Who Treat the Traumatized,* (Bristol, PA: Brunner/Mazel, 1995), 2.

18. Aphrodite Matsakis, *I Can't Get Over It* (Oakland, CA: New Harbinger, 1996), 113.

19. The Four Horses refer to the Four Horses of the Apocalypse found in the Book of the Revelation. The four different-colored horses represent different end time catastrophes. White is conquest, red is war, black is famine/pestilence, and pale is death (Rev. 6:1-8).

20. Germaine Greer, "An African Feast for Flies and Other Parasites," *The Guardian,* Features Section, July 25, 1994, 18.

21. Carol Ostrom, "Our Struggle with Our Hearts," *The Seattle Times,* August 10, 1992, sec.A,1.

22. *Newsweek,* "Christmas Tsunami," front page, http://www.newsweek.com/id/55524 (accessed August 8, 2009).

23. Ibid.

24. Ibid.

25. Daniel Defoe, *A Journal of the Plague Year* (London: Printed for E. Nutt, J. Roberts, A. Dodd, and J. Graves, 1721).

26. Steven N. Gold and Jan Faust, ed. *Trauma Practice in the Wake of September 11, 2001* (New York: Haworth, 2002), 3.

27. Lenore Meldrum, "September 11 and Its Impact on People around the Globe," in *Trauma Practice in the Wake of September 11 2001,* ed. Steven N. Gold and Jan Faust (New York: Haworth, 2002), 65.

28. Ofra Ayalon and Frances S. Walters, "The Impact of Terrorism on Jews in Israel: An Interview with Ofra Ayalon," in *Trauma Practice in the Wake of September 11 2001,* ed., Steven N. Gold and Jan Faust (New York: Haworth, 2002), 137.

Chapter Two

29. Gordon MacDonald, *Ordering Your Private World,* (Nashville, TN: Thomas Nelson, 1985), 13.

30. Archibald Hart, *Counseling the Depressed* (Waco, TX: Word Books, 1987), 41.

31. "Prescription Drug Addiction," University of Alberta, http://www.virtualwellness.ualberta.ca/docs/VW/

MentalIllness/Prescription%20Drug%20Addiction.pdf (accessed May 8, 2009).

32. *Webster's Encyclopedic Unabridged Dictionary of the English Language,* (New York: Gramecy, 1989), 299.

33. Carl R. Rogers, *A Way of Being* (1980; repr. Boston: Houghton Mifflin Harcourt, 1995), 142.

34. Alan E. Nelson, *Spirituality and Leadership* (Colorado Springs: NavPress, 2002), 114.

35. Steve Arterburn and Jack Felton, *Toxic Faith* (Nashville, TN: Oliver Nelson, 1991), 104-105.

36. John O'Neill, "Understanding High-functioning Professionals Who Suffer from Substance Abuse and a Co-existing Mental Disorder," *Houston Medical Journal* (January 5, 2005), http://www.menningerclinic.com/newsroom/ONeillarticle.pdf (accessed October 21, 2008).

37. Eric Marrapodi, "Evangelical Confesses to 'Sexual Immorality' in Letter," *cnn.com*, (November 6, 2006), http://www.cnn.com/2006/US/11/05/haggard.allegations/index.html (accessed November 29, 2008).

38. Gordon MacDonald, *Rebuilding Your Broken World* (Nashville, TN: Thomas Nelson, 1988), 53.

39. ibid.

40. Thaddeus Birchard, "The Snake and the Seraph: Sexual Addiction and Religious Behavior," *Counseling Psychology Quarterly* 17, no. 1 (2004): 84.

41. ibid.

42. Sally Morgenthaler, "Does Ministry Fuel Addictive Behavior?" *Leadership* 27, no. 1 (January 2006), http://ctlibrary.com/le/2006/winter/24.58.html (accessed April 10, 2009).

43. Lyle Schaller, *Discontinuity and Hope*, (Nashville, TN: Abingdon, 1999), 81.

44. *The Columbia Encyclopedia*, 6th ed. s.v. "Ancient hedonism," *Encyclopedia .com*, http://www.encyclopedia.com (accessed July 10, 2008).

45. Standing But Not Operating (SBNO), "Heritage USA: Fort Mill, South Carolina," SBNO, http://sbno.illicitohio.com/heritage/thestory.html (accessed July 10, 2008)

46. Benjamin R. Barber, *Fear's Empire: War, Terrorism, and Democracy* (New York: W. W. Norton, 2003), 216.

47. The course brochure asks the question, "Who Should Attend?" The answer, "This program is for mental health professionals who wish to assist caring professionals deal with the impact of CF. Interested participants may include counselors, psychologists, social workers, psychiatrists, clergy, employee assistant professionals, clinical supervisors and other helping professionals."

48. Annie Besant, *Thought Power: Its Control and Culture* (Wheaton, IL: Theosophical Publishing House, 1966), 101-4.

49. Eric Leigh Schmidt, *Restless Souls: The Making of American Spirituality* (New York: HarperSanFrancisco, 2005).173.

Chapter Three

50. Wendell Berry, *A Timbered Choir: The Sabbath Poems,* (Washington, DC: Counterpoint, 1999)

51. Ken Radant, (course notes, "Introduction to Believer's Church Theology," Associated Canadian Theological Schools, Langley, BC, Fall 2002), 11.

52. Millard J. Erickson, *Christian Theology* (Grand Rapids, MI: Baker Book House, 1985), 21.

53. Christine Sines, (workshop presentation at "Rhythms of Grace For Everyday Life," New Conspirator's Conference, Seattle, WA, March 29, 2008).

54. Daniel I. Block, "Preaching Old Testament Law for New Testament Christians" (paper presented at The National Conference on Preaching, Louisville, KY, March 9, 2004), 5.

55. Mark Buchanan, *The Rest of God* (Nashville, TN: W Publishing Group, 2006), 89.

56. Maurice S. Logan, *Sabbath Theology* (New York: The Sabbath Committee, 1913), 78.

57. ibid. 71.

58. ibid. 188

59. Samuele Bacchiocchi, *The Sabbath in the New Testament: Answers to Questions* (Berrian Springs, MI: Biblical Perspectives, 1985), 77.

60. Meister Eckhart, *Meister Eckhart,* Translated by Raymond B. Blakley, (New York: Harper and Row, 1941). 216.

61. Bruce A. Ray, *Celebrating the Sabbath* (Phillipsburg, NJ: P&R, 2000), 5.

62. Donna Schaper, *Sabbath Sense* (Philadelphia: Innesfree, 1997), 20-21.

63. ibid.

64. Barbara Taylor Brown, *Leaving Church* (New York: HarperSanFrancisco. 2006), 135.

65. Stephen A. Geller, "Manna and the Sabbath," *Interpretation* 59, no 1 (January 2005): 34.

66. ibid.

67. Robert Sherman, "Reclaimed by the Sabbath's Rest," *Interpretation* 59, no.1 (January 2005), 50.

68. Mark Buchanan, *The Rest of God* (Nashville, TN: W Publishing Group, 2006), 88.

69. Abraham Joshua Heschel, *The Sabbath: Its Meaning for Modern Man* (New York: Farrar, Straus, and Giroux, 1951), 14.

70. Barbara Brown Taylor, "Sabbath Resistance," *Christian Century* 122, no. 11 (May 31, 2005), 35.

71. John Stumbo, synchronous chat, George Fox Evangelical Seminary DMin Cohort, March 26, 2007.

72. Wayne Muller, *Sabbath* (New York: Bantam Books, 1992), 82-83.

73. Eugene Peterson, *Working the Angles* (Grand Rapids, MI: William B. Eerdmans, 1993), 66.

74. ibid.

75. Barbara Taylor Brown, *Leaving Church* (New York: HarperSanFrancisco. 2006), 135.

76. "The Offspring of Obedience," *Enrich* (October 2008): 7.

77. Mary Lou Weisman, "The History of Retirement, From Early Man to AARP," *The New York Times*, July 15, 2008, http://www.nytimes.com/1999/03/21/jobs/the-history-of-retirement-from-early-man-to-aarp.html?scp=1&sq=weisman%20history%20of%20retirement&st=c (accessed July 15, 2008).

78. C. Gene Wilkes, *Jesus on Leadership* (Wheaton, IL: Tyndale House, 1998), 22.

79. Annie Payson Call, *Power through Repose* (Boston: Roberts Brothers, 1891), 12-13.

80. Leigh Eric Schmidt, *Restless Souls* (New York: HarperSanFrancisco, 2005), 172.

81. Besant, *Thought Power*, 94-95.

82. Schmidt, *Restless Souls,* 173.

83. *Merriam Webster Online*, s.v. "Worship," http://www.m-w.com/dictionary/worship (accessed November 27, 2006).

84. Schaller, *Discontinuity and Hope*, 57.

85. Eugene Peterson, "The Pastor's Sabbath," *Leadership* 6, no. 2 (Spring 1985): 57.

86. ibid. 55.

87. Gary Preston, "Get a (Balanced) Life," *Leadership* 19, no. 4 (Fall 1998): 54.

Chapter Four

88. "New Doctors Choose Specialties," Doc Zone, http://www.cbc.ca/doczone/ doctors_background.html (accessed January 21, 2008).

89. ibid.

90. ibid.

91. Timothy S. Laniak, *Shepherds after My Own Heart* (Downers Grove, IL: InterVarsity, 2006), 91.

92. Ibid., 57.

93. Joachim Wach, *Sociology of Religion* (Chicago: The University of Chicago Press, 1971), 392-393.

94. Charles C. Manz, *The Leadership Wisdom of Jesus* (San Francisco: Berrett-Koehler, 2005), 4.

95. Walter C. Wright, *Relational Leadership* (Carlisle, UK: Paternoster, 2000), 2.

96. Frank M. Ochberg, "When Helping Hurts," Accessed online http://www.ncvc.org/9-11/main.aspx?dbName=helping_ hurts (accessed July 8, 2009).

97. Anton Wildgans, quoted in Viktor Emil Frankl, *Doctor and the Soul: An Introduction to Logotherapy* (New York: Knopf, 1962), 77.

98. Charles C. Manz, *The Leadership Wisdom of Jesus* (San Francisco: Berrett-Koehler, 2005), 4.

99. Ori Brafman and Rod A. Beckstrom, *The Starfish and the Spider: The Unstoppable Power of Leaderless Organizations* (New York: Penguin Group, 2006), 33.

100. ibid. 164.

101. Know Your Type, "16 Myers-Briggs Personality Types," Accessed online http://www.knowyourtype.com/ (accessed August 20, 2009).

102. Eric Abrahamson and David H. Freedman, *A Perfect Mess* (New York: Little, Brown and Company, 2006), 98.

103. Bill Hybels, *Courageous Leadership* (Grand Rapids, MI: Zondervan, 2002), 84

104. Christian A. Schwarz, *Natural Church Development* (Winfield, BC: The International Centre for Leadership and Development and Evangelism, 1998), 11.

105. Wilkes, *Jesus on Leadership,* 110.

106. Kenneth Boa, *The Perfect Leader* (Colorado Springs: Victor, 2006), 30.

107. ibid. 137.

108. Carly Fiorina, *Tough Choices* (New York: Portfolio, 2006), 5.

109. Robert Greenleaf, *Servant Leadership* (New York: Paulist, 2002), 233-234.

110. Len Sweet, "Dreams Gone Wild: A New Kind of Human" (essay, Gorge Fox Evangelical Seminary LEC06 course materials, Portland, OR, June 16, 2007), 6.

111. During Jesus time on earth leadership was a result of military power (the Romans) or political\religious power (the Pharisees). Jesus presented a different leadership style, one of meekness.

112. Justo L. Gonzalez, *The Early Church to the Dawn of the Reformation*, vol. 1 of *The Story of Christianity* (New York: HarperSanFrancisco, 1984), 96.

113. ibid. 97.

114. Justo L. Gonzalez, *The Reformation to the Present Day*, vol. 2 of *The Story of Christianity* (New York: Harper SanFrancisco, 1985), 245.

115. Earl Creps, *Off-Road Disciplines* (San Francisco: Jossey-Bass, 2006), 99.

116. Leonard Sweet, *The Church of the Perfect Storm* (Nashville, TN: Abingdon, 2008), 14.

Chapter Five

117. Rich Wilkerson, "Theology and Practice of the Baptism of the Holy Spirit," (Pentecostal Assemblies Of Canada (BC/Yukon District Conference on the Ministry, March 3-5th 2008).

118. Len Sweet, *So Beautiful*, (Colorado: David C. Cook, 2009), 29.

119. L. Thomas Holdcroft, *The Holy Spirit* (Springfield, Gospel Publishing House, 1992), 21

120. Millard J. Erickson, *Christian Theology* (Grand Rapids, MI: Baker Books, 1996), 874.

121. Kenneth S. Wuest, *Untranslatable Riches from the Greek New Testament* (Grand Rapids, MI: William B. Eerdmans, 1945), 111.

122. "However, you are not in the flesh but in the Spirit, if indeed the Spirit of God dwells in you but if anyone does not have the Spirit of Christ, he does not belong to Him. If Christ is in you, though the body is dead because of sin, yet the spirit is alive because of righteousness. But if the Spirit of Him who raised Jesus from the dead dwells in you, He who raised Christ Jesus from the dead will also give life to your mortal bodies through His Spirit who dwells in you. So then, brethren, we are under obligation, not to the flesh, to live according to the flesh—for if you are living according to the flesh, you must die; but if by the Spirit you are putting to death the deeds of the body, you will live. [14]For all who are being led by the Spirit of God, these are sons of God."

123. C. Peter Wagner, *Your Spiritual Gifts Can Help Your Church Grow* (Ventura, CA: Regal Books, 1979), 88-9.

124. A. W.Tozer, *Tragedy in the Church: The Missing Gifts* (Harrisburg, PA: Christian Publications, 1978), 22.

125. Ronald F. Youngblood, general editor; F.F. Bruce and R.K. Harrison, consulting editors, *Nelson's New Illustrated Bible Dictionary,* (Nashville: Thomas Nelson 1997).

126. L. Thomas Holdcroft, *The Holy Spirit*, (Springfield, MO: Gospel, 1992), 88.

127. ibid.

Chapter Six

128. Carman R. Berry, *When Helping You Is Hurting Me* (New York: Harper Collins, 1990).

129. Grant Mullen, "Improve your Relationships/Improve your Life," e-book, http://www.drgrantmullen.com/ (accessed May 5, 2009).

130. Eugene H. Peterson, *The Message* (Colorado Springs: Navpress, 1993), 434.

131. Walter Whitely, "Quandries and Queries," Math Central, University of Regina, http://mathcentral.uregina.ca/ QQ/ database/QQ.09.00/teri1.html (accessed November 25, 2007).

132. *Merriam-Webster Dictionary On-line*, s.v. "Balance," http://www.m-w.com/dictionary/balance (accessed November, 25, 2007).

133. Rob Bell, "The Storage Room Meltdown," *Leadership* 26, no. 4 (Fall 2005), 124.

134. Peterson. *Working the Angles*, 2.

135. Judith Valente and Charles Reynard, eds., *Twenty Poems to Nourish Your Soul* (Chicago: Loyola, 2006), 3.

136. Robert S. Hoyt and Stanley Chodorow, *Europe in the Middle Ages* (New York: Harcourt Brace Jovanovich, 1976), 378.

137. ibid. 380.

138. Dallas Willard, *The Spirit of the Disciplines* (New York: HarperSanFrancisco,1988), 158.

139. ibid. 158.

140. ibid. 161.

141. Louis Bouyer, *The Spirituality of the New Testament and the Fathers* (New York: Seabury, 1982), 313.

142. Willard, *The Spirit of the Disciplines*, 191.

143. ibid. 177.

144. Edward J Farrell, *Surprised by the Spirit* (Denville, NJ: Dimension Books, 1973).

145. Bob Sorge, *Exploring Worship* (New York: Bob Sorge, 1987), 65.

146. Thomas Merton, *Contemplative Prayer* (New York: Doubleday, 1969), 34.

147. "Take 21g Idea with 0.0015mg of Salt." *The Age*, February 21, 2004, http://www.theage.com.au/articles/2004/02/20/1077072838871.html (accessed November 22, 2008).

148. Sally Helgesen, *Thriving in the 24/7* (New York: The Free Press, 2001), 22.

149. Watchman Nee, *The Spiritual Man* (New York: Christian Fellowship, 1968), 28.

150. ibid. 75.

151. Stanley J. Grenz, *The Moral Quest* (Downers Grove, IL: InterVarsity, 1997), 248.

152. Joe Friel and Gordon Byrn, *Going Long* (Boulder, CO: VelcoPress, 2003), 23.

153. Kenford Nedd, *Power over Stress* (Toronto, ON: QP, 2003), 131.

154. Sharon Promislow, *Making the Brian Body Connection* (Vancouver, BC: Enhanced Learning and Integration, 2005), 51.

APPENDIX

PROFESSIONAL QUALITY OF LIFE SCALE (PROQOL)

COMPASSION SATISFACTION AND
COMPASSION FATIGUE
(PROQOL) VERSION 5 (2009)

When you *[help]* people you have direct contact with their lives. As you may have found, your compassion for those you *[help]* can affect you in positive and negative ways. Below are some questions about your experiences, both positive and negative, as a *[helper]*. Consider each of the following questions about you and your current work situation. Select the number that honestly reflects how frequently you experienced these things in the *last 30 days*.

1=Never   2=Rarely   3=Sometimes   4=Often   5=Very Often

_____1.   I am happy.

_____2.   I am preoccupied with more than one person I *[help]*.

_____3.   I get satisfaction from being able to *[help]* people.

_____4.   I feel connected to others.

_____5.   I jump or am startled by unexpected sounds.

_____6.   I feel invigorated after working with those I *[help]*.

_____7.   I find it difficult to separate my personal life from my life as a *[helper]*.

_____8.   I am not as productive at work because I am losing sleep over traumatic experiences of a person I *[help]*.

_____9.   I think that I might have been affected by the traumatic stress of those I *[help]*.

_____10. I feel trapped by my job as a *[helper]*.

_____11. Because of my *[helping]*, I have felt "on edge" about various things.

_____12. I like my work as a *[helper]*.

_____13. I feel depressed because of the traumatic experiences of the people I *[help]*.

_____14. I feel as though I am experiencing the trauma of someone I have *[helped]*.

_____15. I have beliefs that sustain me.

_____16. I am pleased with how I am able to keep up with *[helping]* techniques and protocols.

_____17. I am the person I always wanted to be.

_____18. My work makes me feel satisfied.

_____19. I feel worn out because of my work as a *[helper]*.

_____20. I have happy thoughts and feelings about those I *[help]* and how I could help them.

_____21. I feel overwhelmed because my case |work| load seems endless.

_____22. I believe I can make a difference through my work.

_____23. I avoid certain activities or situations because they remind me of frightening experiences of the people I *[help]*.

_____24. I am proud of what I can do to *[help]*.

_____25. As a result of my *[helping]*, I have intrusive, frightening thoughts.

_____26. I feel "bogged down" by the system.

_____27. I have thoughts that I am a "success" as a *[helper]*.

_____28. I can't recall important parts of my work with trauma victims.

____29. I am a very caring person.

____30. I am happy that I chose to do this work.

© *B. Hudnall Stamm, 2009. Professional Quality of Life: Compassion Satisfaction and Fatigue Version 5 (ProQOL). /www.isu.edu/~bhstamm or www.proqol.org. This test may be freely copied as long as (a) author is credited,(b) no changes are made, and (c) it is not sold.*

YOUR SCORES ON THE PROQOL: PROFESSIONAL QUALITY OF LIFE SCREENING

Based on your responses, place your personal scores below. If you have any concerns, you should discuss them with a physical or mental health care professional.

Compassion Satisfaction _____

Compassion satisfaction is about the pleasure you derive from being able to do your work well. For example, you may feel like it is a pleasure to help others through your work. You may feel positively about your colleagues or your ability to contribute to the work setting or even the greater good of society. Higher scores on this scale represent a greater satisfaction related to your ability to be an effective caregiver in your job.

The average score is 50 (SD 10; alpha scale reliability .88). About 25% of people score higher than 57 and about 25% of people score below 43. If you are in the higher range, you probably derive a good deal of professional satisfaction from your position. If your scores are below 40, you may either find problems with your job, or there may be some other reason—for example, you might derive your satisfaction from activities other than your job.

Burnout_____

Most people have an intuitive idea of what burnout is. From the research perspective, burnout is one of the elements of Compassion Fatigue (CF). It is associated with feelings of hopelessness and difficulties in dealing with work or in doing your job effectively. These negative feelings usually have a gradual onset. They can reflect the feeling that your efforts make no difference, or they can be associated with a very high workload or a non-supportive work environment. Higher scores on this scale mean that you are at higher risk for burnout.

The average score on the burnout scale is 50 (SD 10; alpha scale reliability .75). About 25% of people score above 57 and about 25% of people score below 43. If your score is below 18, this probably reflects positive feelings about your ability to be effective in your work. If you score above 57 you may wish to think about what at work makes you feel like you are not effective in your position. Your score may reflect your mood; perhaps you were having a "bad day" or are in need of some time off. If the high score persists or if it is reflective of other worries, it may be a cause for concern.

Secondary Traumatic Stress_____

The second component of Compassion Fatigue (CF) is secondary traumatic stress (STS). It is about your work related, secondary exposure to extremely or traumatically stressful events. Developing problems due to exposure to other's trauma is somewhat rare but does happen to many people who care for those who have experienced extremely or traumatically stressful events. For example, you may repeatedly hear stories about the traumatic things that happen to other people, commonly called Vicarious Traumatization. If your work puts you directly in the path of danger, for example, field work in a war or area of civil violence, this is not secondary exposure; your exposure is primary. However, if you are exposed to others' traumatic events as a result of your work, for example, as a therapist or an emergency worker, this is secondary exposure. The symptoms of STS are usually rapid in onset and associated with a particular event. They may include being afraid, having difficulty sleeping, having images of the upsetting event pop into your mind, or avoiding things that remind you of the event.

The average score on this scale is 50 (SD 10; alpha scale reliability .81). About 25% of people score below 43 and about 25% of people score above 57. If your score is above 57, you may want to take some time to think about what at work may be frightening to you or if there is some other reason for the elevated score. While higher scores do not mean that you do have a problem, they are an indication that you may want to examine how you feel about your work and your work environment. You may wish to discuss this with your supervisor, a colleague, or a health care professional.

In this section, you will score your test and then you can compare your score to the interpretation below.

To find your score on **each section,** total the questions listed on the left in each section and then find your score in the table on the right of the section.

Compassion Satisfaction Scale:

3. ____

6. ____

12. ____

16. ____

18. ____

20. ____

22. ____

24. ____

27. ____

30. ____

Total: ____

The sum of my Compassion Satisfaction questions	So My Score Equals	My Level of Compassion
22 or less	43 or less	Low
Between 23 and 41	Around 50	Average
42 or more	57 or more	High

Burnout Scale:

*1. ___ = ___

*4. ___ = ___

8. ___

10. ___

*15. ___ = ___

*17. ___ = ___

19. ___

21. ___

26. ___

*29. ___ = ___

The sum of my Burnout Questions	So My Score Equals	My Level of Burnout
22 or less	43 or less	Low
Between 23 and 41	Around 50	Average
42 or more	57 or more	High

Reverse the scores for those that are starred. 0=0, 1=5, 2=4, 3=3, 4=2, 5=1

Total: ___

Secondary Trauma Scale:

2. ___

5. ___

7. ___

9. ___

11. ___

13. ___

14. ___

23. ___

25. ___

28. ___

The sum of my Secondary Traumatic Stress questions	So My Score Equals	My Level of Secondary Traumatic Stress
22 or less	43 or less	Low
Between 23 and 41	Around 50	Average
42 or more	57 or more	High

Total: ___

BIBLIOGRAPHY

Abrahamson, Eric, and David H. Freedman. *A Perfect Mess*. New York: Little, Brown, 2006.

Arterburn, Steve, and Jack Felton. *Toxic Faith: Understanding and Overcoming Religious Addiction*. Nashville, TN: Thomas Nelson, 1991.

Ayalon, Ofra, and Frances S. Walters. "The Impact of Terrorism on Jews in Israel: An Interview with Ofra Ayalon." In *Trauma Practice in the Wake of September 11 2001*. Edited by Steven N. Gold and Jan Faust. New York: Haworth, 2002.

Bacchiocchi, Samuele. *The Sabbath in the New Testament: Answers to Questions*. Berrien Springs, MI: Biblical Perspectives, 1985.

Barfman, Ori, and Rod. A. Beckstrom. *The Starfish and the Spider: The Unstoppable Power of Leaderless Organizations*. New York: Penguin Group, 2006.

Barber, Benjamin R. *Fear's Empire: War, Terrorism, and Democracy*. New York: W.W. Norton, 2003.

Bell, Rob. "The Storage Room Meltdown." *Leadership* 26, no. 4 (Fall 2005).

Berry, Carman. R. *When Helping You Is Hurting Me*. San Francisco: Harper Collins, 1990.

Berry, Wendell. *A Timbered Choir: The Sabbath Poems, 1979-1997*. Washington, DC: Counterpoint, 1999.

Besant, Annie. *Thought Power: Its Control and Culture*. Wheaton, IL: Theosophical Publishing House, 1966.

Birchard, Thaddeus. "The Snake and the Seraph: Sexual Addiction and Religious Behavior." *Counseling Psychology Quarterly* 17, no. 1. (2004).

Block, Daniel I. "Preaching Old Testament Law for New Testament Christians." Paper presented at The National Conference on Preaching, Louisville, KY, March 9, 2004.Boa, Kenneth. *The Perfect Leader.* Colorado Springs: Victor, 2006.

Bouyer, Louis. *The Spirituality of the New Testament and the Fathers.* New York: Seabury, 1982.

Brown, Barbara Taylor. *Leaving Church.* New York: HarperSanFrancisco, 2006.Buchanan, Mark. *The Rest of God.* Nashville, TN: W Publishing Group, 2006.

Buchanan, Mark. *The Rest of God.* Nashville, TN: W Publishing Group, 2006.

Call, Annie Payson. *Power through Repose.* Boston: Roberts Brothers, 1891.

Casting Crowns. "Love Them Like Jesus." http://www. christianrocklyrics.com/castingcrowns/lovethem-likejesus.php (accessed March 19, 2007).

"Christmas Tsunami." *Newsweek*, front page, http://www. newsweek.com/id/55524 (accessed August 8, 2009).

Creps, Earl. *Off-Road Disciplines*. San Francisco: Jossy-Bass, 2006.

Defoe, Daniel. *A Journal of the Plague Year*. London: Printed for E. Nutt, J. Roberts, A. Dodd, and J. Graves, 1721.

Doc Zone. "Is your Doctor Taking Patients?" http://www. cbc.ca/doczone/doctors_background.html (accessed January 21, 2008).

Dobson, James. "The Titanic. The Church. What They Have in Common," http://www2.focusonthefamily.com/ docstudy/newsletters/A000000803.cfm (accessed January 25, 2010).

Eckhart, Meister. *Meister Eckhart*. Translated by Raymond B. Blakley. New York: Harper and Row, 1941.

Encyclopedia .com. *Columbia Encyclopedia*, 6th ed. s.v. "Ancient hedonism," http://www.encyclopedia.com (accessed July 10, 2008).

Erickson, Millard J. *Christian Theology* .Grand Rapids, MI: Baker Book House, 1985).

Farrell Edward J., *Surprised by the Spirit*. Denville, NJ: Dimension Books, 1973.

Figley, Charles F., *Compassion Fatigue: Coping with Secondary Traumatic Stress Disorder in Those Who Treat the Traumatized*. Bristol, PA: Brunner/Mazel, 1995.

— — —. "Compassion Fatigue: Toward a New Understanding of the Cost of Caring." In *Secondary Traumatic Stress: Self-Care Issues for Clinicians, Researchers, and Educators*. Edited by B. Hudnall Stamm, 1-20. Baltimore, MD: Sidran Press, 1999.

Fiorina, Carly. *Tough Choices*. New York: Portfolio, 2006.

Friel, Joe and Gordon Byrn. *Going Long*. Boulder, CO: VelcoPress, 2003.

Geller, Stephen A. "Manna and the Sabbath." *Interpretation* 59, no 1. January 2005.

Gold, Steven. N., and Jan Faust., ed. *Trauma Practice in the Wake of September 1 2001*. New York: Haworth, 2002.

Gonzalez, Justo L. *The Story of Christianity*. Vol. 1. New York: HarperSanFrancisco, 1984.

———. *The Story of Christianity*. Vol. 2. New York: HarperSanFrancisco, 1985.

Greenleaf, Robert. *Servant Leadership*. New York: Paulist, 2002.

Greer, Germaine. "An African Feast for Flies and Other Parasites." *The Guardian*. Features Section. July 25, 1994.

Grenz, Stanley J. *The Moral Quest*. Downers Grove, IL: InterVarsity, 1997.

Hart, Archibald. *Counseling the Depressed*. Waco, TX: Word Books, 1987.

Helgesen, Sally. *Thriving in the 24/7*. New York: The Free Press, 2001.

"Heritage USA, Fort Mill, South Carolina." http://sbno.illic-itohio.com/heritage/thestory.html (accessed on July 10, 2008).

Heschel, Abraham Joshua. *The Sabbath: Its Meaning for Modern Man*. New York: Farrar, Straus, and Giroux, 1951.

Holdcroft, L. Thomas. *The Holy Spirit*. Springfield: Gospel Publishing House, 1992.

Hoyt, Robert S., and Stanley Chodorow. *Europe in the Middle Ages*. New York: Harcourt Brace Jovanovich, 1976.

Hybels, Bill. *Courageous Leadership*. Grand Rapids, MI: Zondervan, 2002.

Know Your Type, "16 Myers- Briggs Personality Types," http://www.knowyourtype.com/ (accessed August 20, 2009).

Lanier, Jim. "Take Care of Yourself," *The Journal of Emergency Dispatch* 10, no.4, (July/August, 2008).

Laniak, Timothy S. *Shepherds after My Own Heart*. Downers Grove, IL: InterVarsity, 2006.

Logan, Maurice S. *Sabbath Theology*. New York: Lord's Day Alliance of the United States, 1913. http://www. archive.org/stream/sabbaththeologyr00loga#page/ n7/ mode/2up (accessed August 17, 2009).

MacDonald, Gordon. *Ordering Your Private World.* Nashville, TN: Thomas Nelson, 1985.

———. *Rebuilding Your Broken World.* Nashville, TN: Thomas Nelson, 1988.

Manz, Charles C. *The Leadership Wisdom of Jesus.* San Francisco: Berrett-Koehler, 2005.

Marrapodi, Eric. "Evangelical Confesses to 'Sexual Immorality' in Letter." *cnn.com*, (November 6, 2006). http://www.cnn.com/2006/US/11/05/haggard.allegations/ index.html (accessed November 29, 2008).

Matsakis, Aphrodite. *I Can't Get Over It.* Oakland, CA: New Harbinger, 1996.

Meldrum, Lenore. "September 11 and Its Impact on People around the Globe." In *Trauma Practice in the Wake of September 11 200.* Edited by Steven N. Gold and Jan Faust (New York: Haworth, 2002).

Merriam Webster Online, s.v. "Worship," http://www.m-w. com/dictionary/worship (accessed November 27, 2006).

Merton, Thomas. *Contemplative Prayer.* New York: Doubleday, 1969.

Mitchell, Jeffery T. "Basic Critical Incident Stress Management." (course notes, Courtenay Fire Department, Courtney, BC, December 4-5, 2003).

Morgenthaler, Sally. "Does Ministry Fuel Addictive Behavior?" *Leadership* 27, no. 1. (January 2006). http://www.ctlibrary.com/le/2006/winter/24.58.html (accessed April 10, 2009).

Mullen, Grant. "Improve your Relationships/Improve your Life." Ebook. http://www.drgrantmullen.com/ (accessed May 5, 2009).

Muller, Wayne. *Sabbath.* New York: Bantam Books, 1992.

Nedd, Kenford. *Power over Stress.* Toronto: QP. 2003.

Nee, Watchman. *The Spiritual Man*. New York: Christian Fellowship, 1968.

Nelson, Alan E. *Spirituality and Leadership*. Colorado Springs: Navpress, 2002.

Ochberg, Frank M. "When Helping Hurts." http://www. ncvc.org/9-11/main.aspx?dbName=helping_hurts (accessed July 8, 2009).

"The Offspring of Obedience," *Enrich*, October 2008.

O'Neill, John. "Understanding High-functioning Professionals Who Suffer from Substance Abuse and a Co-existing Mental Disorder." *Houston Medical Journal*, January 5, 2005. http://www.menninger-clinic.com/newsroom/ONeillarticle.pdf (accessed October 21, 2008).

Ostrom, Carol. "Our Struggle with Our Hearts." *The Seattle Times*, August 10, 1992.

Peterson, Eugene. *Five Smooth Stones for Pastoral Work*. Grand Rapids: William B. Eerdmans, 1980.

———. "The Pastor's Sabbath." *Leadership* 6, no. 2 (Spring 1985).

———. *The Message*. Colorado Springs: NavPress, 1993.

———. *Working the Angles*. Grand Rapids, MI: William B. Eerdmans, 1993.

Preston, Gary. "Get a (Balanced) Life." *Leadership* 19, no. 4 (Fall 1998).

Promislow, Sharon. *Making the Brian Body Connection*. Vancouver, BC: Enhanced Learning and Integration, 2005.

Radant, Ken. Course notes from an "Introduction to Believer's Church Theology." Associated Canadian Theological Schools, Langley, BC, Fall 2002.

Ray, Bruce A. *Celebrating the Sabbath*. Phillipsburg, NJ: P&R, 2000.

Rogers, Carl R. *A Way of Being*. 1980. Reprint. Boston: Houghton Mifflin Harcourt, 1995.

Scalise, Eric T. "When Helping You is Hurting Me: Counselor Care Ethics." *Christian Counseling Today* 12, no.4 (2004).

Schaller, Lyle E. *Discontinuity and Hope*. Nashville, TN: Abingdon, 1999.

Schaper, Donna. *Sabbath Sense*. Philadelphia: Innesfree Press, 1997.

Schmidt, Leigh Eric. *Restless Souls: The Making of American Spirituality*. New York: HarperSanFrancisco, 2005.

Schwarz, Christian A. *Natural Church Development*. Winfield, BC: The International Centre for Leadership and Development and Evangelism, 1998.

Selye, Hans. *The Stress of Life*. New York: McGraw Hill, 1976.

Sherman, Robert "Reclaimed by the Sabbath's Rest," *Interpretation* 59. no.1. January 2005.

Sines, Christine. "Rhythms of Grace for Everyday Life." New Conspirator's Conference, Seattle, WA, March 29, 2008.

Sorge, Bob. *Exploring Worship*. New York: Bob Sorge, 1987.

Strand, Kenneth A. *The Sabbath in Scripture and History*. Washington. DC: Review and Herald Publishing Association, 1982.

Stumbo, John. Synchronous chat, DMIN Cohort. March 26, 2007.

Sweet, Leonard. *So Beautiful*. Colorado: David C. Cook, 2009.

_____. "Dreams Gone Wild: A New Kind of Human." Essay in George Fox Evangelical Seminary LEC06 course materials, Portland, OR, June 16, 2007.

— — —. *The Church of the Perfect Storm*. Nashville, TN: Abingdon, 2008.

Swigert, John Jr., James Lovell, and Fred Haise Jr. http://www.phrases.org.uk/ meanings/188425.html (accessed on August 29, 2008).

"Take 21g Idea with 0.0015mg of Salt." *The Age,* February 21, 2004. http://www.theage.com.au/articles/2004/02/20/1077072838871.html (accessed November 22, 2008).

Taylor, Barbara Brown "Sabbath Resistance," *Christian Century* 122, no. 11. May 31, 2005.

Tozer, A. W. *Tragedy in the Church: The Missing Gifts*. Harrisburg, PA: Christian Publications, 1978.

University of Alberta. "Prescription Drug Addiction." http://www.virtualwellness.ualberta.ca/docs/VW/ MentalIllness/Prescription%20Drug%20 Addiction. pdf (accessed May 8, 2009).

Valente, Judith, and Charles Reynard. eds. *Twenty Poems to Nourish Your Soul*. Chicago: Loyola, 2006.

Wach, Joachim. *Sociology of Religion*. Chicago: The University of Chicago Press, 1971.

Wagner, C. Peter. *Your Spiritual Gifts Can Help Your Church Grow*. Ventura, CA: Regal Books, 1979.

Webster's Encyclopedic Unabridged Dictionary of the English Language, (New York: Gramecy, 1989).

Weisman, Mary Lou. "The History of Retirement, From Early Man to AARP." *The New York Times*, March 21, 1999, http://www.nytimes.com/1999/03/21/jobs/ the-history-of-retirement-from-early-man-to-aarp. html?scp=1&sq=weisman%20history%20of%20 retirement&st=c (accessed July 15, 2008).

Whitely, Walter. 'Queries and Quandries." Math Central. University of Regina. http://mathcentral.uregina. ca/QQ/database/ QQ.09.00/teri1.html (accessed November 25, 2007).

Wildgans, Anton quoted in Viktor Emil Frankl. *Doctor and the Soul: An Introduction to Logotherapy*. New York: Knopf, 1962.

Wilkerson, Rich. Pentecostal Assemblies of Canada (BC/ Yukon District) Conference on the Ministry, (work-shop notes) *Theology and Practice of the Baptism of the Holy Spirit*, March 3-5th 2008.

Wilkes, C. Gene. *Jesus on Leadership*. Wheaton, IL: Tyndale House, 1998.

Willard, Dallas. *The Spirit of the Disciplines*. New York: HarperSanFrancisco, 1988.

Woltterstorff, Nicolas. *Lament for a Son*. Grand Rapids, MI: William B. Eerdmans, 1987.

Wright, Walter C. *Relational Leadership*. Carlisle, UK: Paternoster, 2000.

Wuest, Kenneth S. *Untranslatable Riches from the Greek New Testament*. Grand Rapids, MI: William B. Eerdmans, 1945.

Youngblood, Ronald F. general editor; F.F. Bruce and R.K. Harrison, consulting editors, *Nelson's New Illustrated Bible Dictionary*. Nashville: Thomas Nelson, 1997.

CPSIA information can be obtained at www.ICGtesting.com
Printed in the USA
LVOW131943130113

315426LV00001B/5/P